The Grieving Therapist

Caring For Yourself And Your Clients When It Feels Like The End Of The World

Larisa A. Garski, LMFT
Justine Mastin, LMFT
Foreword By Jamie Marich, PhD

16pt

Copyright Page from the Original Book

Copyright © 2023 by Larisa A. Garski, LMFT, and Justine Mastin, LMFT. All rights reserved. No portion of this book, except for brief review, may be reproduced, stored in a retrieval system, or transmitted in any form or by any means—electronic, mechanical, photocopying, recording, or otherwise—without the written permission of the publisher. For information contact North Atlantic Books.

PLEASE NOTE: The examples provided in this book are composites drawn from hundreds of clinical sessions, classes, supervisions, and case consultations. Names and identifying details have been changed to protect the privacy and confidentiality of individuals.

Published by
North Atlantic Books
Huichin, unceded Ohlone land
Berkeley, California

Book design by Happenstance Type-O-Rama

Printed in the United States of America

The Grieving Therapist: Caring for Yourself and Your Clients When It Feels Like the End of the World is sponsored and published by North Atlantic Books, an educational nonprofit based in the unceded Ohlone land Huichin (*aka* Berkeley, CA) that collaborates with partners to develop cross-cultural perspectives; nurture holistic views of art, science, the humanities, and healing; and seed personal and global transformation by publishing work on the relationship of body, spirit, and nature.

North Atlantic Books' publications are distributed to the US trade and internationally by Penguin Random House Publisher Services. For further information, visit our website at www.northatlanticbooks.com.

MEDICAL DISCLAIMER: This book contains material that may be triggering, including references to self-harm, sexual abuse, or trauma. The following information is not intended to replace seeing a therapist or health care provider. Any application of the material set forth in the following pages is at the reader's discretion and is their sole responsibility.

Library of Congress Cataloging-in-Publication Data

Names: Garski, Larisa A., 1986- author. | Mastin, Justine, 1979- author.
Title: The grieving therapist : caring for yourself and your clients when it feels like the end of the world / by Larisa A. Garski, Justine Mastin.
Description: Berkeley, California : North Atlantic Books, 2023. | Includes bibliographical references and index.

Subjects: LCSH: Grief. | Behavior therapists.

LC record available at https://lccn.loc.gov/2022051179
LC ebook record available at https://lccn.loc.gov/2022051180

1 2 3 4 5 6 7 8 9 KPC 29 28 27 26 25 24 23

TABLE OF CONTENTS

FOREWORD	vi
INTRODUCTION	x
1: THE REALM OF OUR PLAGUE	1
2: THE REALM OF OUR HEALTH	28
3: THE REALM OF OUR EARTH	53
4: THE REALM OF OUR ORIGINS	78
5: THE REALM OF OUR KIN	103
6: THE REALM OF OUR REPUBLIC	131
7: THE REALM OF OUR FAITH	160
8: THE REALM OF OUR CRISIS	185
9: THE REALM OF OUR INDUSTRY	213
10: THE REALM OF OUR MEANING	246
GRIEVING SUPPORTS	271
ACKNOWLEDGMENTS	276
NOTES	278
ABOUT THE AUTHORS	291
BACK COVER MATERIAL	295
Index	297

PRAISE FOR
The Grieving Therapist

"Reading *The Grieving Therapist* was like a warm blanket from the dryer—comforting in a way I didn't know I needed until reading it! I learned a lot, but, more importantly, I felt seen, heard, and acknowledged. A definitive resource that everyone in any helping profession needs to read and keep close by, this book beautifully shows the struggles people face and provides real and accessible ways for people to cope. I give this book my highest endorsement and will use it in my courses for professionals."
—SHELLY CLEVENGER, PhD, chair of the department of victim studies at Sam Houston State University

"Garski and Mastin have created a roadmap that supports therapists to show up for themselves compassionately and gently through the grieving process. Full of useful tools, this book helps readers explore the delicate balance between processing personal connections to grief while simultaneously holding space for the client experience. A must-read for all therapists!"
—ERICA HORNTHAL, LCPC, BC-DMT, author of *Body Aware*

"Powerful, relevant, necessary. Reading this timely book is like having a conversation with

the supervisor of your dreams. A refreshing and humbling read for new and experienced therapists alike."
     —NICOLE ARZT, LMFT, author of *Sometimes Therapy Is Awkward*

"There has been a profound lack of support for mental health workers throughout the COVID-19 pandemic and political divides of the last few years. Clinicians have been isolated while trying to hold space for so much suffering. *The Grieving Therapist* mirrors back this collective experience. Through narrative storytelling, creative mindfulness, and hard truths, this book invites readers to compassionately examine their own secondary trauma, burnout, and grief. It invites healers to question the social constructs in which we live and work and to join together to create the world we wish to see."
     —KARINA AYN MIRSKY, MA, ERYT, founder of Yoga Mindset Coaching and author of *Make a Difference and Make a Living Teaching Yoga*

"This book offers clinicians a map and a compass for exploring all dimensions of themselves—in *and* out of the clinical space. Thoughtful and thorough, the authors walk through all that has been shaken by the COVID-19 pandemic and other global upheavals, encouraging the reader to wonder about themselves through metaphors and exercises that support and facilitate healing. Readers can access profound intersections between self and other, self and catastrophe, and self and world to gain an ever-deeper understanding of the ways we experience ourselves. This book is deeply developmentally supportive. I can't recommend it highly enough."

—MARA TESLER STEIN, PsyD, PMH-C, founder and director of The Touchstone Institute for Perinatal Training

"A welcome and much-needed landing spot for bone-weary therapists—like the hug you didn't know you needed until you got it and melted into the embrace. Garski and Mastin do a beautiful job illustrating the challenging, awe-inspiring, and often terrifying topography of grief both in and outside the therapy room. This book will guide you toward not only understanding how and why we're grieving as a collective, but also how to navigate your own grief as a helper and as a human. This is a must-read for any therapist who wants to encounter, honor, and give space to their own grief, so that they might make room to accompany others as they grieve, too."

—MEGAN KELLY, MA, owner of Informer Coaching & Consulting and "Antiwork Therapist" on Instagram

"The information and validation shared in *The Grieving Therapist* reminds us that we must care for ourselves with as much zeal as we offer our clients. As a clinician in the field of trauma therapy, I especially appreciated the examples to bring support into my daily life. And I've gained a new appreciation of the challenges involved in supporting students as they return to campus ... and mentees as they work to establish themselves as professionals in this new, post-pandemic culture. Learning that I am not alone in these challenges was supportive in and of itself. I highly recommend *The Grieving Therapist* to my clinical colleagues, fellow educators, and anyone in the health care industry who has made it through the pandemic and is still on their feet. Much gratitude to both Justine and Larisa for the gentle reminder to reach out to our community and allow them to hold us while we too grieve."

—KATHRYN TEMPLETON, LPC, C-IAYT, Ayurvedic practitioner and director of the Ayurvedic Yoga specialist program at Yoga International

*For death, who reminds us to live
In gratitude to our communities who support us
and
In memoriam to Meronym, who died
while we wrote this book*

FOREWORD

"I never want to help another person ever again for as long as I live!" I cried out in the early summer of 2022.

As a clinical counselor and operator of a large training company in eye movement desensitization and reprocessing (EMDR) therapy who manages scores of team members plus our therapist students, from day 1 of the COVID-19 lockdown I stayed optimistic and operated in fierce worker-bee mode. I proudly lived by the motto *if you don't adapt and swim, you will sink and die,* so even as I continued to take care of myself the best way I knew how, I wasn't fully relating to the struggles of my colleagues, or indeed of many of the people I served. I largely dissociated from my own feelings about the world crumbling in around me by working and taking care of others—one of my default settings as a human. Then a series of personal life transitions, which included an unexpected move and learning to live with a new partner, coupled with the demands of running a business in our current climate, caused me to hit a wall. I thought: *Why the hell am I doing this to myself? I'm just going to burn it all to the ground and go and set up a fruit stand on a beach highway—maybe in Hawaii, maybe in Croatia—just somewhere far away from here.*

And then I got an email from Justine Mastin asking me if I would write the foreword for this book! I chuckled, ever amused by the universe's sense of humor. Clearly this is a book that I personally needed to read during this season of my life, and I am so glad I did. And I am even more excited that other therapists will benefit from its wisdom at this time in history, when truth-telling is a lost art, yet is so desperately needed.

A mutual friend and colleague introduced me to Justine in 2016. After I saw what she created with YogaQuest and other creative ventures, I became a top member of her fandom (pop culture community). I then met Larisa in 2021 when the two of them collaborated on writing their book *Starship Therapise*, and my expressive artist soul beamed with excitement when I realized what these two were putting out into the world. And I was so glad to learn that there are other therapists who are out and proud about their creativity. For it is creativity that is needed to work with the most complex of cases that we see in our practices, and it is creativity and expression that will fuel the revolution that our field needs to heal itself.

Justine and Larisa write with a great deal of whimsy while also not shying away from the hard subjects of what makes being a therapist in the modern era so hard. They take on the perils of dealing with insurance, the rigid structures around training and formation, and how, as natural caretakers, we are vulnerable to being overworked in the name of doing the right thing.

I shook my head in agreement so many times as I read *The Grieving Therapist,* even shouting out "Preach, preach!" a few times. Yet the motifs and metaphors they used also caused me to ponder how I most want to spend my time as a person and as a creative being on this planet.

And as if the universe couldn't get enough of her own sense of humor, I contracted COVID-19 in August 2022 as I was reading through *The Grieving Therapist.* Having managed to avoid the illness for over two years, I ended up having an experience similar to what Justine writes about in this book. As I navigated my own several weeks of hell with COVID, I was grateful to know I was not alone in what I was feeling. Today I'm grateful to both Justine and Larisa for their vulnerability in this work. I've long taught that therapists and people in positions of power need to be more open about their human struggles, because so many of us think we are bad therapists and thus bad people for having very human experiences. Embracing our humanity is the key to embracing our wholeness, and when we can accept this challenge, everyone around us can ultimately benefit.

Grief is messy and complicated, and it can tie you up in knots, particularly when one has to navigate many different layers of grief. Even Elisabeth Kubler-Ross acknowledged that "the five stages—denial, anger, bargaining, depression, and acceptance—are a part of the framework that makes up our learning to live with the one we lost. They are tools to help us frame and identify what we may be feeling. But they are not stops on some linear timeline in grief."[1]

Justine and Larisa do not shy away from the mess—they dive right in to name it and to explore it. And that's why this book is what our field needs right now. Thank you both for telling the truth. Through this lost art of truth-telling we stand a chance of unraveling the knots and healing our shame.

—Jamie Marich, PhD, LPCC-S, REAT, RYT-500

INTRODUCTION

They say there's good grief
But how can you tell it from the bad?
Maybe it's only in the fact,
Good grief's the one that's in your past

—DESSA[1]

We tried to write this introduction so many times. But how do you introduce grief? In a top hat and tap shoes (Justine's choice)? Perhaps you go retro and quote Emily Dickinson: "After great pain, a formal feeling comes" (Larisa's choice). You could zoom out to the macro and lean into the longevity of our global grief—rising sea levels, hundreds of thousands dead from a pandemic, ineffectual government—or you could zoom in incredibly close and go micro with a personal anecdote.

After so many rewrites, we must admit, we found ourselves feeling aggrieved. Ain't that just the way? Grief is many things; it brings terror and tears and gifts in shitty wrapping paper. It has zero fucks to give about timing. So even though the timing of this introduction finds us personally and professionally bereaved, we're going to do our best to find some humor in the pain and some joy in the pathos. To paraphrase one of our personal favorites, Carl Jung: you know you're really alive when you're feeling all of it—the good, the bad, and the ugly. Therapy, like life, should contain all of it. And since this is a book by therapists for therapists, then this book also needs to contain all of it. Or, to paraphrase a client, it needs to be properly life-y.

The truth is that there is no right way to start because this isn't the beginning of a story; it's the middle. We are all still living inside the trauma, not reflecting upon it from some future place. So, reader, we join you in the middle of our grief, which we will lay out for you like a map. This feels appropriate, as maps themselves have no beginning and end; they simply are, and there are a multitude of routes to take across them. There are indeed many roads to the summit.

But before we dive into the life of this book, we need to check our mapmaking supplies and review our provisions. To put this in purely scholastic terms, we're going to offer a note on theoretical orientation, a summary of structure, and a perspective on self-disclosure, and we'll conclude with a word on methodology. This journey into grief will take us into uncharted territory for which there are yet no complete maps. But together, reader, we hope to draft a guidebook.

A Note on Theoretical Orientation

This is not an academic text, though it is a book informed by the work of many academics and researchers in the fields of marriage and family therapy, psychology, counseling, education, posttraumatic growth, and philosophy. And we do hope you find it useful in the classroom. In creating this book, our goal was to both invite and evoke grieving emotions for you, the reader, and to cocreate a supportive community within which you can sit and practice being present with such intense feelings as pain, joy, despair, hope, sadness, fear, and anger. While this book is informed by the work of many—Vanessa Machado de Oliveira Andreotti, Audre Lorde, Søren Kierkegaard, Michael Ende, and Janina Scarlet, to name just a few—the researchers and work we chose to directly incorporate into each chapter are grounded in their ability to evoke feelings, including (perhaps most especially) those uncomfortable feelings and experiences you may have been avoiding for months, if not years. We've pulled thinkers from across fields of study ranging from activism to Zen.

Our intention is for this book to be an experiential journey into your own grieving. Therefore, don't be surprised if this book doesn't mention your favorite research or journal articles. We've chosen our sages for the impact they've had on the world around them, the general zeitgeist, and/or on us, the authors. These thinkers are, as are we all, imperfect humans, who we believe have important messages to share with you in your time of grieving—even when that important message is anger. We have included each thinker's cultural and/or ethnic heritage in an effort to normalize the variety of humans who have contributed to our collective experiences, both conscious and unconscious.

We share all of this in advance, not to frighten you away from this book but rather to help you make an informed choice. Although this book is meant to challenge, it's also meant to delight. Play, which entails imagination, jokes, puns, and riddles, helps us build cognitive flexibility. It allows us to express our feelings without getting too attached to any particular outcome or result. It can also do the simple but mighty task of eliciting a smile, which is something all too rare in our field in these times. To help create a sense of play, we use the framing device of you, the reader, embarking on your own hero's journey to explore and map the ten realms of grief: plague, chronic illness, planet, family, community, politics, faith, crisis, industry, and utopia. The hero's journey, while imperfect in its construction, speaks directly to the challenging and cyclical nature of grief. Woven through each chapter you'll find creative mindfulness vignettes that use metaphor and wordplay to evoke and describe what might be your experience in reading this grieving book.

A Summary of Structure

Each chapter addresses one of the ten realms of grief. In each realm, you, the reader, will encounter one or two researchers—sages, if you will—who offer guidance in first feeling and then making sense of the grief found in that realm. You may choose to take all, some, or none of the guidance offered. In keeping with our framing device of mythic storytelling, you may find some (or all!) of the guidance irritating, lacking, or downright wrong. The meaning or map you make in each realm is very much your own. Our recommendation is to be present with your feelings and to attempt to be curious. But even this you may decline. As the authors of this book, we see ourselves as guides rather than experts. In keeping with the tradition of narrative therapy to which we, the authors, most definitely belong, you, reader, are the author of your own experience, which very much includes the experience of reading all, some, or none of this book.

Each realm includes a section called "Grieving Tools" where we'll share with you a tool we have used in our own personal and clinical practices to aid in our own grieving and in the grieving of our clients. The section will present ways to use this tool within the therapy space to support your clients as well as ways to use this tool outside therapy as you move through your own personal grieving process.

The second half of each chapter addresses the impact each realm of grief has on specific relationships within the world of therapy: the relationship between the therapist and themselves (self of the therapist), the relationship between supervisee and supervisor,[1] and the relationship between student and teacher. Each chapter will conclude with a meditation on the impact that realm has on what we see as the most primal of relationships: the relationship between death and love.

A Perspective on Self-Disclosure

In the same way that we mindfully choose which parts of ourselves we share with clients, we mindfully chose what to disclose throughout this book. Rather than handing you pieces of our own grief to hold, our self-disclosures are

---

[1] When we speak of supervisees and supervisors, we're using our marriage and family therapy (MFT) lens, and your particular licensure may vary in the language it uses. For clarification, "supervisees" are those who have finished their studies and are working toward their licensure, also called the preclinical or prelicensure period. "Supervisors" are those who oversee preclinical supervisees, or they may also be managing a clinical staff.

examples of ways in which we have navigated aspects of the realms of grief. Thus, we invite you to take the meaning or metaphor that resonates, and to leave the tales that fall flat.

Because we'll be sharing aspects of our own personal stories within the pages of this text, we think it's important for you to know a bit about our background. We, Larisa A. Garski and Justine Mastin, the authors of this book, are systemic and relational thinkers—marriage and family therapists by trade—which means that we take a dialectical view of the world. We see individuals as existing in constant conversation with and relationship to other social groups or systems. We are also narrative therapists who practice a specific kind of narrative therapy: through using narrative therapy and play therapy, with the integration of pop culture—or, as we like to think of it, modern mythologies—we created a style of therapy that we lovingly call Therapeutic Fanfiction. We outline this modality in our previous book, *Starship Therapise: Using Therapeutic Fanfiction to Rewrite Your Life.* [2] Although this book takes more of a scholastic approach to grief, you will still find accessible stories woven through the text. Below, we include details about each of us that you may find relevant as you read this book:

Larisa was raised among sled dogs. These experiences during her formative years affected her in a variety of ways, not the least of which is that she leads with her nose and registers the smell of a place or a new experience simultaneously with the look or shape of it. Larisa's family lineage is rooted in Eastern Europe. Poverty and religion plagued both her maternal and paternal lines for generations. Larisa finds internal clarity and compassion in rebuilding her connection to the land of her forebears.

Justine was raised by the television. Her most foundational attachments were to the characters she loved, which placed modern mythologies at the forefront of her spiritual life. Justine is a cisgender woman of both Western European and Eastern European descent and is Jewish on her mother's side (in the Jewish tradition, this means Justine is considered fully Jewish). She considers herself culturally Jewish and feels an ancient connectedness to the Jewish people. Justine is also an experienced registered yoga teacher at the two-hundred-hour level. Though mostly retired from yoga teaching, during the years she worked as a yoga teacher trainer she devoted portions of each training to exploring the problematic and colonial aspects of yoga's dissemination in the United States. Thus, you'll find some yogic references in this book.

A Note on Methodology

This book exists within the broad context of qualitative research. The methodology or doing of this book came from our own clinical experiences as practicing therapists and supervisors. This book was informed by our personal experiences as both supervisees and supervisors. Both Larisa and Justine have been students inside and outside the halls of academia, and Justine is now an educator very much within said halls. Finally, this book is a product of the conversations and collaborations we've had with each other and with other colleagues as we continue to face the horrors of climate collapse, pandemics, and political unrest.

Welcome

You've made it through the introduction and now find yourself on the brink of joining us in the realms of grief. For your courage so far, we thank you. We're going to make this ride, if not joyous, then at least varied. We invite you to read at your own pace and rhythm, meaning that you might start with the introduction and then head straight to chapter 5. We encourage you to meet this book where you are and to start, stop, reroute, and proceed as needed, but perhaps always with caution. No doubt the road is perilous. But you do not grieve alone. We, your authors and colleagues, walk alongside you.

1

THE REALM OF OUR PLAGUE

> *It was maps that made it possible for me to dream those other worlds up and imaginatively transport myself to other places.*
> —MICHAEL WHITE[1]

As Michael White and David Epston, the Australian and New Zealander founders of narrative therapy, very well might have said: all journeys begin with a good map.[2] While we don't know if Michael and David were fans of video games, our imagined versions of this dynamic duo—that is, our *headcanon,* to use a bit of fandom lingo referring to imagined versions of a known reality—most certainly are. So when we channel their love of maps, we conjure an image of them as guides in the video game of our lives, presenting us with our very first dungeon map. But because this is real life and this is a real book, there is no map to the therapy realms of grief. We must craft the map together, and in so doing enact our own healing and our own meaning.

Our journey begins in the Realm of Our Plague—a place of germs and despair. Your surroundings at first seem like a desolate wilderness, and you are a weary traveler beset on all sides by tribulations, with nary a friend or companion in sight. But just as it begins to feel as if all hope is lost, you peer through the trees—such a dark shade of green that they almost appear black—and make out a dim spark of orange. With cautious optimism, you walk toward this flash of orange, and with each step the spark grows brighter. After a while, your ears prick at the sound of laughter and human voices. How long has it been since you've gathered with others in community?

"Oh look, another arrival!" calls a voice from up ahead. You step into a clearing with a blazing campfire in the center, surrounded by many inviting faces. As you stand awestruck and overwhelmed, a tall, bearded fellow hands you a steaming mug, while another member of the community makes room around the fire. "Welcome to therapist base camp," your new friend says as you sit down and begin the introductions.

This is the therapy community. They, and you, have already been through a terribly tricky trek, and now you are finally joined together to share in the journey to come. Take a moment and consider what you want to share with this community about your solo sojourn to base camp. What were the years of pandemic like for you, both as a person and as a therapist?

Terrors of Telehealth

For us, the authors, the pandemic years were painful. Our solo sojourns were mapless, as are all first adventures. And there were no guides to give us even their own hand-drawn maps. We were all truly explorers, and none of us by choice. We started charting our course across the sea of teletherapy unguided. While there may be those rare therapist birds out there who were practicing in a predominantly virtual manner prior to the COVID-19 pandemic, for most therapists this was a brand-new experience. Offices were suddenly left with many an abandoned house plant to watch as dust gathered on once frequented, but now deserted, desks and silent sofas. Piles of magazines accumulated outside doors, and space-rental bills caused silent weeping.

We found ourselves in the unenviable position of having to explain concepts like social distancing and airborne transmission before we fully understood them ourselves. Our clients turned to us for knowledge and reassurance that we simply did not have. All of us, regardless of therapeutic modality, were thrown into a situation where our clients suddenly knew more about our struggles than we ever thought possible, simply because we were all going through the same global pandemic together.

And we were doing it in the leaky boat of telehealth. Justine hated this new reality. She did not adapt well to the new way of working. Her home was not set up for it, and she had a beautiful office space—for which she was still paying rent—sitting empty. When clients asked Justine how she was doing, she would answer: "We're in a pandemic!" And clients would nod knowingly. It was a fool's errand to pretend that any of this was okay. Justine found that clients appreciated her disclosure that she wished she was in the office getting a LaCroix from the mini-fridge, rather than passing her partner in her own kitchen during breaks. The irony is that although Justine initially hated working from home, she has now made the hard decision to give up her space and will likely never return to a brick-and-mortar facility for clinical practice. It took the better part of the first year of the pandemic for her to adapt, but once she created a cozy space to work in her home, she found that working remotely suits her multiproject-filled lifestyle.

This was not everyone's experience. Many therapists found themselves struggling to make the impossible work, learning that virtual play therapy was as oxymoronic as it sounded. While on one of her ubiquitous COVID walks, Justine ran into a social worker neighbor who described doing virtual sandtray therapy with children as "the most boring video game ever." Many more found themselves pressured by practice owners or community mental health administrators to return to the office sooner than felt safe, while others pushed to return to "normal" as soon as possible. For those first six months of 2020, everything just felt wrong. Notice what comes up for you when you think back to those initial weeks and months. Can you remember when the message was that the lockdown would be for two weeks, and then four, and then six? And how you felt when it moved to an indefinite length of time?

At the time of this writing, we find ourselves two and a half years into the COVID-19 outbreak. Many therapists have become more practiced at virtual therapy, but that doesn't mean teletherapy is equivalent to in-person therapy. Adaptation is not always synonymous with functionality. We are all experienced at coping, and we do it well. And yet, we remember what it was like before. If you are a new clinician or a student who does not have this memory, your body still knows that this is not quite right. Your body probably alerts you to this fact in a variety of ways, and we'll talk more about this in the section on education.

We're no longer sitting in rooms together with one another's nervous systems. Humans were built to live in community, and that means physical community. We (the authors) are big fans and proponents of the online world and the healing power of our online and fandom attachments, which is to say our one-way emotional connection to fictional or celebrity characters.[3] Yet even we are feeling the impact of the lack of personal emotional connection with other living beings.

During the first year of shifting to telehealth, we would often joke with clients about only seeing one another from the mid-torso up. As a therapist who talked with her hands as much as with her words, Larisa had to adjust to the narrow lens of the camera. No longer able to use her body language to model shifts in focusing when working with couples and families, Larisa found herself narrating aloud where her gaze was focusing. Justine tried for a while to create the feeling of being in the office by setting up an elaborate system so that the camera pointed at her full body in her chair, but it got too complicated (so many wires). Ultimately, both Larisa and Justine found that they had to let go of parts of their previous clinical styles to adapt and fit into the teletherapy box.

As frustrating as this state of affairs was, perhaps some of you found ways that virtual therapy brought you gifts, like the ability to wear hot pink stretchy pants or fidget with a fidget cube under your desk while actively listening. Even if you weren't a person who fidgeted during a session before, you likely discovered that it is difficult to hold the same kind of attunement via telehealth without a fidget.

The nature of telehealth allows for greater emotional space between client and clinician because you aren't together in the same physical space, experiencing the crushing weight of client emotions. For some clinicians, the emotional remove inherent to virtual sessions provided a welcome relief. These clinicians found that teletherapy made it easier for them to be compassionately present without being empathically flooded by the client's feelings.

In Office, in Pain

For those of you who continued to work in office or in person, this presented its own unique challenges. Our colleagues shared a number of these challenges with us. The first and most obvious is that they were afraid for their safety. The pandemic was still largely misunderstood, and they couldn't be sure if the measures being taken could keep them safe. Less known, perhaps, is the guilt they felt about not wanting to go to work. Much of the world's population was out of work, and they were still gainfully employed, but they didn't want to work in this way. So when they talked to loved ones about their fears, they were often met with responses like "at least you have a job," which made it hard to get the emotional support they so desperately needed.

Those who were able to work virtually still struggled with the guilt of having a job that could transition to a virtual space that allowed them to stay safer than their friends, family members, colleagues, or clients who had to choose between quitting their jobs and becoming unemployed, or going into work and putting themselves at risk. For therapists, like so many folks in the helping professions—such as teachers, doctors, nurses, and home health aides—there were no good choices; just a series of painful options to sit with and choose from as best they could, with an ever-increasing sense of isolation and dread.

Perhaps you experienced the strain of being a caregiver for someone who was ill, or caring for a loved one who was immunocompromised and for whom you were in constant fear. Caregiving is stressful and complicated work under the best of circumstances; caregiving during the plague was certainly not the best of circumstances. Caregivers were isolated from their usual support systems, and both reprieve and relief were either in short supply or nonexistent, leading to caregiver fatigue. Many people who cope with caregiver fatigue experience feelings of guilt and shame about being exhausted with their loved one. If this was a part of your experience, we invite you to take a breath and make space for self-compassion for all that you were asked to do under such unbearable circumstances.

See yourself again around the fire, held in caring community with friends, colleagues, and kind strangers. As you look around the circle, you might notice empty spaces—empty cushions and stools. Not everyone survives the Realm of Our Plague. Some of us did not survive the journey. This is an invitation to remember those who, like you, did not have a map and who were unfortunately consumed by what they did not know lay ahead. As humans of old believed, beyond the known world lay monsters. And it is also an invitation to keep map-making and journeying in the ways that you choose. It is in community that we grieve; if we insist on going it alone, only sadness waits for us. Or, to quote our headcanon of Michael White and David Epston: "A community of mapmakers is always going to make a better map."

Part of the struggle of the COVID-19 pandemic is the way it isolated us from one another. In the flurry of efforts to remain safe, many of us prioritized physical safety over emotional safety. This statement is not a stick with which to beat ourselves; rather, it's a magnifying glass with which to investigate. This will not be our only chance to use these skills. As humans continue to impinge upon the habitats of animals, bringing us closer to diseases for which there are no cures, our experiences of plagues will likely be many and varied. If these words resonate with you, we invite you to use the subsequent sections as an opportunity to reach out and rebuild. We have only just begun to process the pain of our COVID-19 plague. As every therapist knows, we can only do so together.

Around the Campfire

During the course of writing this book, Justine caught COVID-19. She was triple vaccinated (the standard at the time), but the variant of the moment caught her unawares. We've talked a lot in this chapter about the changes in working because of the pandemic, and now we talk about the changes in working because of the disease itself. When Justine began to feel poorly one day, she assumed it was a cold—she was vaccinated, after all. But in this story, like so many you have heard before or perhaps experienced yourself, it was not a cold. The at-home test immediately and alarmingly read "positive." A follow-up with a rapid test confirmed the result.

Justine was in a state of shock. Because she lives with severe asthma, contracting a disease that targets the lungs was terrifying, as were all of the unknowns. As of this writing, science is still unsure of the pandemic's long-term impact on the body, although there have already been reports of folks dealing with long-term physical, emotional, and cognitive issues colloquially referred to as long COVID.[4] After her diagnosis, a tearful Justine called Larisa and relayed her fears: "I've had hundreds of colds, and dozens of bronchitises and laryngitises and sinus infections, and even a pneumonia or two.

But I've never had COVID, and I don't know what's going to happen. I'm scared."

Even though she had counseled several clients through receiving a COVID diagnosis and had talked through similar fears with them, it wasn't the same as feeling it viscerally in her own body. Justine discovered that the "brain fog" she'd heard many folks describe felt more to her like an illness-induced ADHD/depression combo, with a mild aphasia. She literally could not focus, and she canceled her appointments for the week following her initial positive diagnosis. Luckily, clients were understanding. But after the acute illness, the symptoms didn't stop. The illness-induced cognitive and emotional symptoms persisted, as did a fatigue that would come on suddenly and profoundly. For weeks, working with clients was excruciating. As a proponent of appropriate therapist self-disclosure, Justine was forthright with clients about what she was going through, and sometimes she needed to cancel a planned session at the last moment when the fatigue hit.

To try to calm her nerves, Justine reached out to her online community to ask about others' experiences with COVID. She discovered that, now that she was "in the club," friends and acquaintances would disclose to her certain realities of COVID-19 recovery that they hadn't previously shared. For one thing, this illness, like all illnesses, is not a binary experience. One is not sick and then better. Rather, one is sick and then in various degrees of sickness and health. In the event that you haven't been aware of this, reader, we want you to know that a lack of awareness on this issue is understandable. This information is not appropriately disseminated, and as with all Western medicine, doctors and news outlets lean into the binary; but the reality is always somewhere in the gray.

Let us return to the campfire. As you sip your hot beverage, you and your compatriots share your experiences weathering the COVID-19 plague. A fellow camper-clinician shares their experience as a disabled person, explaining: "I've always had to be aware of plagues, or what I suppose those who are privileged with strong immune systems would call 'low-grade plagues.' Every year when flu season starts up, I live in fear because if I get the flu I could die. When folks compare COVID to the flu as a justification for getting back out into the world, I feel furious. In the beginning, I hoped that COVID might shine a light on what it is to be immunocompromised and disabled. I hoped there might be a mainstream cultural shift toward greater compassion for folks like me. But mostly that just hasn't happened. I feel torn between just giving into bitterness or full empathy exhaustion."

You nod and give this camper a comforting look. You might offer them the affirmation that you do see them and you do hear the ways in which this twenty-first-century plague was uniquely hard for them.

The bearded camper who greeted you when you first arrived nods at the camper who just shared and offers, "You know, to be honest with you, I was a bit of a COVID minimizer. I mean, I knew it was real, but I had to go back into the office. I'm a day-treatment therapist, and there just was not the option to go virtual. I suppose it was my way of making sense of something that didn't make sense, just so I could go on. I really did need to think of COVID as something manageable or at least survivable, like the flu. Because otherwise I would not have been able to get out of bed and go to work in the morning. And I had to go to work. I'm from a very poor family. I have no social safety net. If I don't go to work, it means my cat Juniper and I won't eat. I am sorry. I see now that making that analogy to the flu was insensitive." You watch as these two campers nod at one another.

Across from you, a camper wearing hammered gold hoops clears their throat. "You know, for me, it's complicated. I'm not a fan of the oppression Olympics, and I'm not interested in comparing pain. And, yet, as a person of color, things were rough for my community. They were harder for Black and Brown folks for so many reasons, not the least of which had to do with institutional racism, lack of resources, and higher rates of poverty. I look around this fire and I see all this pain. But, you know, at my practice where I work with a diverse group of clinicians, my clients were the first to be hit hard with

COVID-19. I counseled a person who watched half their family die of COVID during the first month of the pandemic. And I know it hit all of you. But we were hit first, and we were hit harder. I'm angry. I'm sad. I want to be heard."

There is a palpable silence around the campfire. You witness several campers struggling with their own feelings and their own memories. You pause and notice your breathing as your own memories and emotions bubble to the surface. You take several deep breaths and try to come back to one of the core messages your compatriot offered: *And I know it hit all of you. But we were hit first, and we were hit harder. I'm angry. I'm sad. I want to be heard.* You turn and make eye contact with your colleague and say: "I see you. I hear you." You listen as this sentiment is slowly echoed by each person sitting around the campfire.

Then another camper speaks: "I've been afraid to speak up because I had economic privilege during the pandemic. And still do. I work, but it's very part time, and my partner has always worked from home. So we didn't have to even go through the logistical nightmare of shifting offices and making do in a cramped space. But I'm a mom of a small child who couldn't get vaccinated once vaccines were available. I was so scared that I would get sick and bring it home. And people were so mean to me about it. They told me I was overreacting and that if I was vaxxed, and my partner was vaxxed, then we'd be all good. Typically my mom would watch my daughter when we both had to work, but mom refused to get vaccinated, so we had to put her in day care, something we'd never done. And there were sick kids all the time! It felt like nobody cared about me or my daughter."

You and your fellow campers exchange comforting words, and the tea is passed around one last time. After a few moments of silence, a camper in a bright pink hat turns to you and asks: "What about you? What has your experience been?" You meet her eyes and smile sadly. You take a deep breath and begin to share.

Grieving Tools—The Neutral Zone

Whatever your experience of the pandemic, likely there are beloved others in your life who felt or acted differently than you would have hoped. So as you prepare to leave the realm of the pandemic and embark on the next phase of this journey with us, we offer you *the neutral zone*. This tool invites you to reenter the space you share with people with whom you might have been fighting or at odds during this challenging time. We want to be clear that we are not trying to get you to accept or condone your loved one's feelings or choices; we are simply inviting you to enter into a practice of neutral noticing.

The concept of the neutral zone—inspired by the *Star Trek* universe's region of demilitarized space between the feuding Romulan Empire and the Federation—invites you and your clients to explore ways to navigate toward neutrality. This is a space where you can both rest and explore future courses of action without embracing or even accepting the family member who called you out on social media for choosing to get vaccinated, for example.

Client

A solid indication that it might be time to visit the neutral zone is when you start to notice strain in either yourself or in your client's language and behavior. When the therapy system is straining to find positive meaning or reaching for systemic reassurance that either does not feel reliable or does not feel present (or both), it might be time to invite your client to pause, breathe, and practice both noticing and naming those events and feelings that are currently participating in a sense of distress. Depending upon how your client responds, you may use this opportunity to engage some relational questions, shifting into exploring opportunities to make meaningful connections in ways that feel both sustainable and safe. The neutral zone can seem like a place to enact change. But as *Star Trek* fans know, the neutral zone is not a place for action or reaction so much as it is a place for conversations and reflection. When you notice you or your client attempting to shift back into change-making talk, you might want to pause and normalize this desire for change while honoring the very real truth that noticing is itself an act of change.

Therapist

Now let's shift just to you and your life outside the therapy room. The tool of the neutral zone when applied outside the therapy space means something slightly different. For you, the therapist, we invite you to both notice and take an emotional step back from all your current feelings and struggles so you can sort them out. One of the most common complaints we heard from our colleagues during discussions we had in preparation for this book was the pervasive feeling of being overwhelmed and flooded. We aren't asking you to ignore or compartmentalize these feelings, but we are inviting you to label those noticings that belong to your job as a therapist and those noticings that belong to every other aspect of your life on planet Earth. Therapising during a pandemic made the pandemic feel incredibly pervasive and inescapable. But in order to be effective therapists, we must take breaks from our therapist role. The neutral zone invites you to shift out of your space as an active healer and into your role as a fellow human being. This differs from classical compartmentalization in that you aren't putting away your experiences as a clinician so they're out of sight and out of mind. Rather, you're getting emotional distance from your clinical experiences to make space for all the other experiences of your life.

Due North: Self of the Therapist

While for most of us COVID-19 was our first experience therapising during a plague, it's unlikely that it will be our last. This is a hard message, and an important one. To pretend that the world will return to a prepandemic normal is actually harmful. This idea encourages us to believe in a fantasy that is just that—a fantasy. We, the authors, are firm believers in the importance of fantasy, but when we don't acknowledge that some hard truths are fact, we can fall into magical thinking and a host of other cognitive distortions. By acknowledging the pain caused by the COVID-19 pandemic, as well as the likelihood of continued variants and other plagues, we allow ourselves the opportunity to grieve and to mindfully plan. We must first acknowledge and study the terrain before we can add it to our map. Maps change and thus need to be revised periodically.

In order to manage our expectations of what comes next and to foster healthy and sustainable adaptation to this brave new world of COVID variants, we must sit down with our sadness and loss. Luckily, you can sit in the light of the campfire around which we, your fellow therapists, all sit. What parts of therapising did the pandemic take from you? What losses are you grieving?

We, the authors, invite you to spend some time with your own expectations and fantasies. If you recognize parts of yourself that want things to be different, that makes sense. The reality is that none of us have fully grieved for what has been lost—not just the loss of human life, which is immense, but the loss of our identities as therapists; the loss of how and where we worked; and the loss of the diversity of work we once did. During the first months of the pandemic, and still at the time of this writing, our practice is centered around collective trauma.

There was once a time when at 11a.m. we would work with someone dealing with anxiety around being in open spaces, at noon we'd see a couple navigating their engagement, and at 1p.m. we'd see a client coping with a depressive episode. Now, and especially early in the pandemic, this has become an 11a.m. client struggling with anxiety around the pandemic, a noon couple fighting about when or even whether they can have a wedding, and a 1p.m. client depressed about the pandemic. We were and are exhausted from having the same conversation over and over and over again. For many of you, this may speak to one of the greater losses of the COVID-19 pandemic: where once you found joyful purpose in your therapy work, now you find only exhaustion. Though recognizing this is likely painful, we invite you to make space for this exhaustion around the campfire. You're surrounded by fellow clinicians who also once loved this work and who now instead feel buried in fatigue. Look around the fire and see not just your fellows, but their exhaustion as well. There are many entities around the campfire and they're all here for healing.

Due West: Supervision

For those who were supervisees in 2020, you were unprepared for what awaited you, as were we all. For Justine, she had just taken on a new graduate-level intern right as the pandemic took hold. This intern only got the experience of being in the office for a couple of weeks before the office had to shut down. Her entire practicum experience with Justine was online. This is one story that echoes so many more. There are clinicians practicing today who have never worked with a client in person. Not to mention the compounded stress and strain for those who were attempting to get fully licensed during this time and struggling with what often felt like immense application delays, perpetually canceled and rescheduled licensure exams, and inadequate exam technology. Wherever you are on this continuum, chances are this is not how you imagined working as an emerging therapist would be. The grief you hold around the loss of the dream of practicing how you wanted is valid.

For supervisors, this shift created a new road for which there were no maps. As a guide, you were asked which way to go, but without the map, you were only guessing. You likely felt pressure from supervisees who needed guidance in how to hold big emotions that you yourself were also struggling to manage. It took months to settle into a semblance of a rhythm, and as our world continues to struggle with religious, political, environmental, and viral upheavals, it continues to be challenging.

Even in the beginning of the COVID-19 pandemic, there was opportunity for growth and connection. Larisa, who provides supervision to supervisees as well as managing a clinical staff of twenty to thirty clinicians, recalls weekly conversations in which she "verbalized to normalize;" that is, she named her struggles with exhaustion, despair, and burnout. This invited her colleagues to put down their emotional burdens and share with one another the confusion and turmoil surrounding them. As the pandemic progressed, Larisa observed a shift in many of her clinical team as they reached out with requests for more virtual activities that, when offered, were attended either sparsely or not at all. Of course, this makes sense, too. They didn't want another opportunity to sit and stare at a virtual screen; they wanted a campfire in the woods. We all wanted in-person community. Being a leader of any kind during the first years of the COVID-19 pandemic meant holding space for others to ask for things that you were rarely in a position to give. Sometimes it also meant being the messenger of bad news: *We have to shut down the office. We don't know if insurance will cover virtual sessions. No, the HIPAA-compliant video chat software is not working well. Yes, we are still waiting on claim reimbursement. I don't know when things will change.*

If any or all of these scenarios feel familiar to you, we invite you to remain present with your feelings. If you notice feelings of regret or remorse, we invite you to make space for them around the fire without trying to judge them or analyze them or rationalize them. You did the best you could. After all, this was your first global pandemic.

Due East: Education

If you were a student in 2020, that was a tough time to be in therapy school. You were also in the unenviable position of witnessing firsthand as your faculty and staff scrambled to find a way to keep the school operating. And you had to cope with the uncertainty of whether or not you would be able to continue your education. Perhaps you even questioned whether it made sense to continue, given all that was going on in the world. Or perhaps the pandemic lit an even bigger fire beneath you to get out there and help. Whatever was happening inside you and within your cohort makes sense. Once classes transitioned to an online format, students had difficulty adapting. Justine witnessed a cohort turn on itself. The students couldn't regulate their emotions, so they tried to hand those feelings to one another. It was a microcosm of what was happening out in the world.

If you were a teacher, perhaps you weren't trained in or prepared for online teaching, and the learning curve may have been steep. Your students never looked you in the eye anymore. Or maybe they did—how would you know?! You had to pivot from your original curriculum. With students not in the room together, group work, role plays, and all sorts of other activities had to be changed. You made it work. We see how you made it work and how you did your best under the worst of circumstances. We also know that the students didn't necessarily see or appreciate that, and that isn't their fault. The dysregulation in their nervous systems was profound and inconsolable. It took not just teaching acumen but deep therapeutic skill to hold space for student emotions on top of educating. And not all those who taught before the pandemic stayed in that role once the plague arrived.

Due South: Death and Love

How did you make meaning through the first years of the COVID-19 pandemic? Part of how we, the authors, made meaning was through our love of stories, which offered feelings of hope and useful language related to the grief we were facing. The TV show *WandaVision* provided us just that opportunity. Perhaps the show's famous and beloved quote from Vision, Wanda's husband, is already materializing in your mind: "What is grief if not love persevering?" As Wanda, the title character, moved through the messy wasteland of her grief following the death of her family, she hurt people—not because she was trying to hurt them, but because she was so consumed by her own pain. For therapists, part of what makes grief so terrifying on a personal level is that we work according to that most basic of healing dictums: first, do no harm. If we're consumed by pain, how can we still avoid doing harm? We can't. Usually we turn the harm inward and hurt ourselves to keep from hurting our clients. This dynamic can take numerous forms, such as overbooking yourself with clinical hours and then having no emotional energy left to share with your personal community; pushing through any type of physical pain to be present in a session that results in increased pain hours later when your workday has finished; and not taking breaks during your clinical work day.

In the yogic tradition, there is a *yama* (duty or observance) called "ahimsa," meaning "do no harm," just like the healing dictum mentioned above. But rarely do we consider that harm to ourselves is still harm. So we invite you to pause and consider your own ahimsa. Is it pointed only outward? Or is it like the Force from *Star Wars*, both around us and within us? If we find that our grief is harming us instead of our clients, it's still causing harm, and we must make our own peace with it before returning to the clinical world.

We suggest that the beginning of that peace is found in Vision's quote referenced above. Whenever we grieve, it's because something we love has died—a person, a home, an ideal, a belief system, or something else dear to us. The pain we feel comes from the love that remains after what we loved has ceased to exist in its once-beloved form. As therapists, we've all lost the way we used to practice. Even if you're new to the field and started practicing during the pandemic, you lost the dream of how you wanted to practice. The sadness we feel is equivalent to the love we once felt in the Before Times as practicing therapists. As you sit with this sadness and pain, we invite you to remember this love because it will be the emotion that helps you to change in a way that continues to honor that love.

This is where ritual enters our conversation. Ritual is a vital part of meaning-making; it allows us to both let go and hold on to what was lost. We invite you to consider designating a talisman, or an object of power, to represent what was lost. For example, Justine took many items from her former office and now keeps them in her home office, as a reminder of what was and what still is. Larisa, her clients, and her supervisees have found healing familiarity in the ritualistic way she opens each session with the question "What do you need today?" and closes each session with "Do you have what you need?" This practice creates a sort of linguistic talisman. It cannot be held, but rather, it holds a brave space.

Pause for a moment and consider what your object of power could be—something that symbolizes what is past that you can carry forward with you in a new way. There is no wrong answer. There is only what is resonant for you. Once you find that something, we invite you to choose its placement wisely and consider it regularly.

Being a therapist during a global pandemic is a situation for which none of us were trained. Depending on when you're reading this book, you might finally have access to graduate courses or at least continuing education courses that focus on practicing during a global catastrophe. For those of us on the front lines of the COVID-19 pandemic, all we had was each other.

As you look around the campfire and into the eyes of your beleaguered colleagues, you realize that you need guidance, or at least a map with which to venture forth. You share this musing with your compatriots, and one of them observes that there are no maps for the realms of grief. To which the pink-hat-adorned camper replies: "Then we shall make them!" She jumps up and begins passing out journals and all manner of writing utensils. "We can each catalog the regions we visit, and at the end we can compare our results," she says. "By the end, think of the detailed map we will have to offer future travelers!"

You look down at the journal in your hands and turn to the first page. Let us begin.

2

THE REALM OF OUR HEALTH

As a living creature I am part of two kinds of forces—growth and decay, sprouting and withering, living and dying, and at any given moment of our lives, each of us is actively located somewhere along a continuum between these two forces.

—AUDRE LORDE[1]

Audre Lorde was a self-proclaimed "black woman warrior poet"[2] during the trials and tribulations of the latter half of the twentieth century. While many remember her as an activist who valiantly fought for the rights of people of color, queer folks, and women, she was also an early advocate in the realm of chronic illness, which refers to any ongoing medical condition that requires daily care and support.[3] Diagnosed with breast cancer in 1978, Audre spent the next decade of her life navigating the dialectic between health and illness.[4] As she so poignantly states in her book, *The Cancer Journals*: "My visions of a future I can create have been honed by the lessons of my limitations. Now I wish to give form with honesty and precision to the pain faith labor and loving which this period of my life has translated into strength for me."[5] Audre's words light the way as we venture into our next region, the Realm of Our Health—a place of duality and complication, where you will need both caution and curiosity as you chart the terrain.

After a reflective evening with your fellow campers, you arise in the morning feeling refreshed and invigorated. Many of the campers are off to other realms, and you bid them goodbye with waves and well wishes as they shoulder their packs and head out into the forest. A few of your fellow hikers remain, and you decide to go together deeper into the woods to explore the next realm in this continent of grief. Sunlight filters through the pine trees and a hush falls over the forest as you and your friends saunter along. After some miles the trees begin to clear and the canopy opens. A lovely pond stands before you. You and your companions decide to rest here for a midmorning snack.

You walk along a narrow dock that juts a few meters out into the pond, and you sit down on the edge, swinging your feet back and forth above the water. As you stare into the looking glass of the pond, you notice a sense of stillness and quiet. You're amazed by the lack of flies and mosquitoes; this truly feels like a magical place. As you look across the water, you notice the birds and small creatures at the edges of the pond. You think you spot fuchsia feathers on one and bright purple plumage on another. Your gaze drifts back to the still waters, and you notice several meters away an iridescent fin. It must belong to a fish! Slowly, you remove your hiking boots and socks and dip first one then the other foot into the cool water. You watch the ripples each foot makes, slowly moving outward.

A hazy afternoon sun yawns in the middle of the sky. There is nowhere else but here that you need to be. This place is peaceful, so you are serene as you sit. You begin to check in with your physical body and notice how it feels. As you breathe into this noticing, you remember the last years of your work as a therapist. You might recall the perpetual tension of those first few months of the pandemic when your neck, shoulders, and jaw could never just relax. You might remember the worry that sat in the pit of your stomach, causing pain and indigestion. Perhaps you recall congestion that lingers or brain fog that never quite seems to dissipate. As you blink your eyes you might recall the strain from screens and exhaustion—the eye twitch that persisted for months. You've been through so much.

And perhaps you already had pains or other bodily struggles before the pandemic, and they were exacerbated by your more recent challenges. You may have already dealt with migraines. Perhaps you already had insomnia or joint inflammation and the accompanying pain. If you had chronic illnesses such as severe asthma, cystic fibrosis, diabetes, endometriosis, kidney disease, multiple sclerosis, ulcerative colitis, or cardiac concerns you already had to be cautious of infection well before the dawn of the COVID era. You managed the ebb and flow of both physical and mental symptoms in a world that still largely treats illness as a polarized dichotomy of wellness or illness. All these journeys are inscribed within your flesh and bone.

Lost in a reverie, you barely notice the iridescent shimmer gliding toward you in the water.

The Dance of Health and Illness

There is a tendency to talk about health and illness as if there were only two possible states: that of the completely and totally well, whose skin glows like the summer sun and whose limbs can sprint up mountains, and that of the sick, whose body is a shade of green and whose limbs can barely carry them to the kitchen, let alone up the block to the pharmacy. These are inaccurate stereotypes that do not in fact comprise all the nuanced experiences of being alive. A healthy body is not, as mainstream discourse would have you believe, a body of a particular size or shape. If you move through the world in a bigger body, then you are all too familiar with the dismissive stares and the medical stereotype that larger bodies are sicker bodies.

In reality, health and illness constitute a duality that we all possess and experience—often simultaneously. For example, within Justine's physical body there is a constant dance between areas that feel physically strong and agile and areas that are painful and constricting. These conflicting states exist for a variety of reasons: severe asthma, decades-old dance injuries, and more than four decades of life, to name a few. But one partner does not overtake the other. Both partners in this dance require equal time, though some need more care at certain moments. When the weather turns colder, the illness partner and wellness partner may begin to get out of step, and then they need some dance lessons.

Consider for a moment your experiences with this dance between wellness and illness. This can include your experience of any disabilities in your body. A *disability* is a medical or physical impairment that limits your ability to engage in daily life tasks.[6] If your immediate reaction is that you have no illness or disability, let us pause. The cultural discourses that govern our conceptions of health and sickness are many and varied. In mainstream American culture, morality and productivity are involved in this dialectic. Productivity is prized, so speed is valued over taking one's time, whether to recover from an illness or to sit by a pond and reflect.

In terms of morality, mainstream American culture continues to walk the path laid down by the Puritans, who viewed illness and physical aberrations such as left-handedness as sinful and weak. To be healthy is to be strong and good, hale and hearty. In cultures where generational poverty has been present, illness is seen as a weakness and a threat to survival. Folks often delay going to the doctor until the last possible moment, due in part to financial constraints but also due to mental constraints: denial is the tool they have to cope with illness and pain. Why bother calling the doctor when they're only going to prescribe a treatment you can't afford? If you're situated at some of the bigger intersections of marginalization, illness brings with it the threat of not being believed by doctors and thus having your problems be moralized and not taken seriously. For the Black, Indigenous, and people of color (BIPOC) community, memories of a not-so-distant past where they were abused in the name of medical research loom large, and inequities in the treatment of BIPOC communities are still common, leading to a great mistrust in the American medical system.[7] We invite you to consider how you view illness and wellness as well as the systems that interact with these states, such as private health care, the modern medical system, pharmaceutical research, and pharmaceutical manufacturing.

If you move through life with a chronic illness or a disability, and especially if you're also a person with an additional marginalized identity, then you're already all too familiar with the limitations of the medical system detailed above. You've likely sat in meetings and been expected to hold space for colleagues as they opine about the struggles of sitting on hold with insurance providers as they attempt to refile a client claim, silently seething as you think about all the time and energy you already spend on hold working with insurance to get your *own* medical needs met so you can then sit on the phone with insurance providers as part of your job. So many of the struggles of the chronically ill go unseen, in part because they often aren't observable. How many times have you heard variations on the phrase "well, you don't look like you're sick/tired/in pain"?

If you do have a disability that's visible to the general populace, then you must face the stares or averted gazes and sit with either the pity or the disgust sent your way—none of which you asked for, and likely none of which is particularly helpful to you. Even those systems ostensibly designed to be of help or service to you often miss the mark. Audre Lorde tells of the harrowing experience of going to a follow-up treatment with her oncologist while feeling "that brave new-born security of a beautiful woman having come through a very hard time and being very glad to be alive,"[8] only to be told by the attending nurse that she needed to put back on her prosthesis to hide the absence of her right breast, because being visibly one-breasted was "bad for the morale of the office."

When you navigate any type of chronic condition, you feel constant pressure from mainstream society to just conform—to just try to look like everyone else. This pressure comes in many forms, not the least of which is the current wellness industrial complex,[9] exemplified by private businesses such as Goop, DoTerra, CorePower Yoga, and Moon Juice. It is not our intention to shame you if you happen to enjoy a CorePower Yoga class, one of Goop's lip balms, or an elixir from Moon Juice. However, if you have felt left out, called out, or shamed by these private businesses, then we intend to stand with you and validate your experience.

These businesses all market a specific view of health and wellness: a lithe, strong body that can be achieved solely through the independent consumption of products and workout classes. They perpetuate stigma against larger bodies as being sicker or weaker. The implication here is that if you do not have this type of "healthy" body, that is solely due to your own lack of money and motivation. Thus, health becomes an individual rather than a systemic issue about which an individual can either feel shame or pride, depending on the results of their work ethic and the contents of their bank account.

The other system that greatly influences our feelings around wellness and illness is the system of the family. How were you raised to conceptualize health and sickness?

As you stare into the still waters of the pond, you may notice a variety of memories and feelings bubbling up within you. Lost in thought, you barely register the splash of cool water on your forearms. You turn to your right and see a member of the merfolk—their iridescent tail slaps the water, and this time you are drenched by a deluge of water. Soaked to your skin, you sputter and cough as the merperson silently chuckles. You pull a towel from your rucksack and begin to dry off while you keep a careful watch on the merperson. As they swim to the center of the pond, you notice that they seem to float through the water, causing only the faintest of ripples. Neither human nor fish, the merperson is exactly what they are: a merperson. They are an embodiment of a *dialectical relationship*. The human part and the fish part are forever in conversation, moving into and out of synthesis. They contain both human and fish, and are incomplete one without the other. You consider your own well-being and are suddenly struck by the duality that lives in your own body. You are not entirely well nor entirely ill. You are both, and that makes you whole. You wave a thank-you to the merperson, who smiles and winks before diving deep into their watery home.

La Vida Es Dolor

As therapists, we know that life is painful. Pain can be challenging to express, making it difficult for others to understand the pain we're feeling. Pain is often only visible through how our bodies react to it, but depending on the person viewing our reactions, this can still be perceived as "faking it" or "being overly dramatic." Many folks with chronic illness describe how friends and family lose patience with them, failing to understand why the person with the illness can do some things and not others. Chronically ill folks get the opportunity to practice being with pain more frequently than the average human being. Sometimes family members will reject those struggling with chronic illness or choose distance over presence because the pain reminds them of their own, which can also be a reminder of their own mortality. Nobody wants to be reminded that one day they will die. For some, it feels easier to consider a chronically ill friend or family member to be the "other" than to recognize their own discomfort and fear of death.

In her journey through the realm of health, Audre Lorde often reflected on the relationships between death, pain, and life. She wrote about how her cancer diagnosis and the ensuing pain nearly broke her, causing her, for a time, to lose her sense of self.[10] As part of her recovery, she chose to make space for this pain, and as it ebbed, she chose to use her struggles with death as an opportunity to broaden and deepen her perspectives on life, love, and family. The closer we are to the pain of death, the closer we are to discovering what it means to each of us as individuals to live fully. Perhaps at this point some of you are thinking: "That's all well and good, Justine and Larisa. But when I'm doubled over in pain due to endometriosis, I'm not feeling closer to my reason for being. I'm about to pass out and need someone to give me a Coca-Cola Classic." To this we say: "Precisely." When you're consumed with pain, you need a caring community to support you, and you need time to let the feelings of pain pass, and then you need still more time to recover from all that painful feeling you were doing for hours and hours and hours. Then and only then can you, like Audre who walked this path before you, find the meaning within your pain and the unique truth of what it is to have a meaningful existence.

Perhaps you've noticed the pattern? Throughout this book, we are extolling the importance of reflection time—a necessary component of the meaning-making of most grieving models as well as posttraumatic growth. Yet time is the very thing our modern age often denies us. All the technological advances that are supposed to free up our time have only succeeded in creating more tasks for us to do.

Years ago when Larisa was working under supervision, she had a supervisor who expressed gratitude for Larisa's chronic illness. Larisa remembers her supervisor saying: "I'm glad you have asthma. Asthma forces you to stop." At the time, Larisa was in the midst of recovering from yet another asthma flare-up and the ensuing month of illness, and she found her supervisor's words to be shocking and hurtful. Larisa hated and resented her asthma—how could this person who cared about Larisa be grateful for this lifelong illness that had caused her so much pain? Larisa's supervisor appreciated a truth that Larisa herself would later come to understand: asthma was an external force equal in strength to both late-stage capitalism and Larisa's desire to do good and meaningful work in the world. Without asthma, Larisa likely would have spent decades attempting to be the most productive therapist without giving much time or thought to her life outside of work. Asthma forced Larisa to sit for long hours at a time. Asthma forced her to practice presence with her illness and her feelings. Eventually Larisa's struggle with asthma would allow her to become a cherished guide to Justine as she struggled with her own diagnosis.

Grieving Tools—Defining Limits

Necessity is the mother of invention. The limitations posed by illness, disability, and chronic illness need not be barriers to a full and wondrous existence. Sometimes our expectations of greatness can prevent us from getting creative with our limitations. A slogan that has served Justine well in various aspects of her life is: if you can't do something well, do it really, really poorly. Whether creating art or taking care of herself, sometimes the best Justine can do is to do the thing really poorly. It's a start to figuring out how to fit the thing into her life.

You might be familiar with sandtray therapy, which is based on the simple act of playing creatively in a sandbox. Before successful creative play can begin, the sandbox needs a frame—that is, sturdy walls joined at the corners to keep the sand in. Our human limitations give us the structure we need to create and play. The sky should not be the limit; we need an actual limit. This is how we discover the meaning of life.

Client

Sandtray therapy and other play therapies are useful not just for children but also for teens and adults. Structured play allows for the confines of the therapy room and the tools that are available, and it invites the imagination to fill in the gaps of what's missing. When clients are grieving physical limitations, whether caused by a traumatic accident, illness, or genetics, it can be helpful to invite them to think expansively about what their physical limitation *offers* them. While this is likely not the therapeutic intervention you lead with, it can be helpful once the client feels validated and normalized in their grief, which in itself takes time. There are often opportunities or beneficial surprises within the constraints of illness. Perhaps a client met their partner through a support group for their illness, or they were able to heal discord with family through hospital visits. Limitations spark creativity. When one can't use their legs, they discover new ways to move through the world; when one can't see, they discover new ways to embrace their environment; and when one has difficulty breathing, they discover how they need to move and rest in order to survive. It's normal to grieve for what is lost or not present, and there's also an opportunity to identify the gifts inherent in this unique human experience.

Therapist

Being a therapist in these times means you'll find yourself faced with a plethora of limitations on how you can practice. This is an invitation to get curious about how you can care for your well-being within the constraints of modern life. As previously mentioned, Larisa has severe chronic asthma. Among the many things this entails, Larisa's diagnosis means she is immunocompromised. During the first part of her clinical career, Larisa worked with children and families. She found this work to be profoundly rewarding. However, she was also sick with some manner of cold, flu, or ear infection all the time.

For folks who work with children, conventional wisdom holds that after the first year of getting sick with everything, you'll be immune; but this was not the case for Larisa. Still, she wanted it to be true. After several years and a series of progressively worse illnesses that culminated in another bout of pneumonia, Larisa—under the advice of her friends, colleagues, and medical team—had to face the reality of her limitation: her asthma would not allow her to work with children. In the years since leaving pediatric psychotherapy, Larisa has found great purpose in *inner* child work with her teenage and adult clients. Though she still sometimes mourns the loss of her work with children, she finds both meaning and hope in bringing her experiences and skills with children to her work with adults.

Due North: Self of the Therapist

Since we're dealing in dyadic constructs, let us acknowledge a fundamental truth: what we call something is not equivalent to the thing itself.

We use language and classification systems as crude measurement tools to help us make sense of and make meaning from the world of life that exists both within us and around us. So, for example, when we talk of the Self and the body as if they were two separate things, we do so in an attempt to understand them. But it's crucial to understand that they're integrated parts of the greater system that is you. Descartes was onto something when he said, "I think, therefore I am." His conception of the mind as separate from the body was a stepping stone on the scientific road to create tools that would go on to help us to treat illness like never before. But it also set humans on a path of compartmentalization from which we have yet to fully recover. Over a century later, Bessel van der Kolk[11] would show us that the mind, though powerful indeed, is inextricably linked to our bodies, which carry the record of our living experiences. We separate to reintegrate.

As therapists, we often focus our work on using our brains and our emotional bodies. But as we know, so much of our own pain is stored in our bodies. Consider for a moment whether you're fully existing in your body right now, or if you have chosen separation as a way to protect yourself from feeling. Just notice, without assigning any judgment to what you find. If you've made the Cartesian separation of mind and body, consider whether you can sit in your body for a moment. If that's too uncomfortable, that's all right. Being in the body is often uncomfortable, not just because of how your body feels but because of how you feel about your body.

Western society communicates many messages about what it means to have a body—which bodies are worthy of compassion and which are not—and how our bodies should function and look. It's very difficult to keep those messages from filtering in, and it can seem easier to avoid feeling that body than to live in its pain. But our bodies know when we're ignoring them or hating them. We'll talk more about the complex internal communication within our minds and how bodies are not a unitary being in chapter 4. For now, consider the things you think about your body, and imagine what would happen if you told another person you thought those things about *their* body. Would that person still want to engage with you? And how would you feel, having said that to another person? We're guessing you would never say those things to your fellow human. Even if you've had similar conversations with clients ad nauseam, where are you with having this conversation with yourself?

We feel grief for not being allowed to embrace the body we had while growing up. We grieve having to be in conflict with our bodies because of what society and our families told us about our bodies. We may still carry remnants of hurtful looks and conversations, insults read or overheard. These feelings can be overwhelming, and as clinicians, we know all too well that human beings tend to avoid what feels overwhelming. If this state of overwhelm is resonating for you, then we invite you to think about the support you need in order to start to be with this sadness and pain. The more you can show up for your own experiences related to chronic illness, disability, and pain, the more ready you'll be to hold compassionate space for your clients when they bring these concerns into the therapy space.

Due West: Supervision

If you are a supervisee, you may need additional training and support around topics of chronic illness and disability, including but not limited to the training you receive in supervision. While continuing education is an integral part of your growth as a clinician, we invite you to sit with the power of *parallel processing*, which occurs when you and your client are going through similar events or emotions at the same time, each influencing the other. The more you can sit with your own physical body and get curious about the relationship you have between wellness and illness, the more you'll be able to hold compassionate space for your clients as they learn how to get curious with their own bodily systems. Notice what's happening in your own body right now. If you're having a visceral feeling, that's all right. Just notice what's coming up for you. Consider that this might be how a client feels when you bring up the importance of their body. You can use the power of this parallel process to better inform your therapeutic work. You are now more informed of your clients' worldly experience. Suddenly your experience and scope of practice expand. Experiential learning is taking place, even at this very moment.

Supervisors, consider for a moment where you are on your journey to accepting the duality of wellness and illness in your own body. Now consider how you feel about bringing this into the supervision space. As we know, not nearly enough time in therapy school is devoted to the physical form of our clients and ourselves. Supervisors have yet another challenging opportunity to help their supervisees understand which parts of their clients' bodily experiences are within their scope of practice, and which are not. Supervisors can gently remind supervisees that they need not take the place of their clients' doctors (which would clearly be outside the realm of appropriate psychotherapy practice). They need only to invite and support their clients in learning how to listen to their bodies' messages and to advocate for themselves with others. Practicing and building distress tolerance around bodily messages applies both to the therapist-client dyad and to the supervisor-supervisee dyad.

As is often the case when talking about the physical being in America, this is an opportunity to help your supervisees build skills around shame. When discussing the body, a supervisee may express feelings of guilt and shame for lack of training or anxiety related to scope of practice. If some of what's coming up for you around bringing this up in the supervisory relationship is around "scope of practice," that makes sense. It's not uncommon for therapists to feel as though their scope of practice is the brain and only the brain. But as we know, the brain lives in the body; so this is well within your scope. Be mindful when working with supervisees that this will likely also be new territory for them, and make sure to get conversational consent before bringing this into the supervision space.

Due East: Education

Students, you have a body. It probably isn't brought up very much in school, but there it is, clear as day: you, with a body. Your body is part of your experience of moving through the world and it's part of your experience with your clients. Your clients will look at your body and have thoughts and feelings about it. We know it's uncomfortable to think about that. And yet, students, you are complete human beings. You bring with you to your studies all parts of you, the sick and the well. The reality is that graduate school isn't set up for folks with chronic illness and disabilities. Despite efforts to the contrary, lesson plans and even classrooms are created for folks who have average physical, emotional, and cognitive functionality: a person who has four limbs and can use them all without any type of aid or support, who can use all five senses, and who can feel and think even when exposed to moderate external stress.

Although schools attempt to offer accommodations, in our experience, teaching staff don't always respect these policies or even know about them. There may not be malicious intent here, but rather the consequence of teachers and professors being woefully underresourced and overburdened (not to mention underpaid) in academia. So if you're a student who requests an accommodation, the burden is on you to follow up with your instructors to make sure your accommodation request is read and to ask what their plan is to implement it. This is additional work placed upon you that is simply not part of your averagely bodied peers' experiences. We validate the unfairness of this entire series of experiences. If you aren't satisfied with your instructor's response to your request, you can take it up with your school's disability services department or your department chair. We know this feels scary, but we want to remind you that you have every right—both ethically and legally—to have your accommodations met. We also want to acknowledge the time, effort, and money that these types of self-advocacy require. We invite you to reach out to trusted supporters to help you navigate this often labyrinthine process and to craft a plan that feels right for you. This plan might involve less challenging the system and more external resourcing to just get through grad school.

Whether or not your school has talked to you about the care and feeding of your body, we invite you to spend some time on this. You matter. Yes, even as a "lowly" graduate student. The social constructs around suffering students—the beliefs that sleepless nights, eating snacks for dinner, and sitting in a chair for twelve hours a day are normal parts of grad school—need to be questioned as well. In both master's-level and doctoral programs, professors and graduate school systems tend to foster the Nietzschean idea that what doesn't kill you makes you stronger, which is to say that pain is a necessary part of graduate training. In reality, there's no reason for someone to undergo hazing and be beaten down before they even enter the field. This is how we lose good prospective therapists.

Teachers, you use your bodies for the education of the next generation of therapists, and we're guessing it's tired. You might experience this teaching fatigue on top of your own chronic illness or disability journey. However you're coming to this conversation, we invite you to take a moment to think about the curriculum you're working with and to consider whether you're discussing the importance of your students' bodily experiences with them.

This is currently an area for growth in most graduate schools for a number of reasons, not the least of which is that it's uncomfortable to talk about. Many educators are still struggling with their own bodily experience and don't want to stir up discomfort in their students that they will need to hold. We understand that. We invite you to consider how you might bring up with students the importance of acknowledging and being curious about their future clients' bodily experiences, and also to tell them how to bring the conversation around bodies and social constructs into the therapy room. If nothing else, please consider talking to your students about environmental accessibility. For example, it's not enough for an entryway to comply with the ADA; do your students know that they need to have armless chairs in the waiting room for clients of size? Also, is your classroom set up for folks with various chronic illnesses and disabilities, and are accommodations available for students to access?

We know that so much is asked of you, teachers, and that we're asking for still more. We see how you attempt to enact change within systems that are slow to move. That said, when students have accommodations granted by disability services, it's vital that you read the description of them, understand them, and connect with the student about them (when possible and appropriate). Universities are based on a socially constructed norm of students that only represents some of the students we serve. While teachers often deal with their work by leaning into structure and strictness, we invite you to lean into compassion and offer patience and grace to your students and yourself.

Due South: Death and Love

The sun glares hot and strong as you blink your eyes. You look around and realize that the cool morning light has shifted into the heat of midday. Where did the time go? And where is the merperson—fish?—you think you saw moments ago? You stare at the still waters of the pond and notice a flick of an orange tail. You peer down below the dock and notice a small school of koi fish lazily swimming in circles. You find yourself wondering yet again just how long you were meditating. You shake your head and begin digging through your rucksack. Now seems like as good a time as any to sketch out a map of this region—the Realm of Our Health and merfolk?

Chronic illness brings us closer to the realization of our mortality. Perhaps this is part of why caring for ourselves and each other around the issue of illness can be so challenging. If you aren't ready to face your own mortality, then you likely don't enjoy receiving ever-present reminders. And yet leaning into the care and maintenance of our physical being can be an opportunity to engage in both self-compassion and self-love. Each time we take our medications or do our physical therapy, we have a choice. We can decide that this is a burden and look at it as such, a reminder of our impending end, or we can acknowledge that care for our physical form is in fact the middle of the story—the part of the story where we are the sages who support our friend, the body, in its needs. We can care for it as it cares for us. Our bodies do everything within their power to keep us alive, so in our moments of nurturance, we're returning the favor. While we might tend to think of the individual person as singular, the reality is that there are many living parts that make up a human being. We are a galaxy for our cells. By caring for the many thousands of cells that make up our physical being, we are caring for ourselves.

3

THE REALM OF OUR EARTH

> *The cosmos is also within us. We're made of star-stuff. We are a way for the universe to know itself.*
> —CARL SAGAN[1]

Talking about the fate of the world is nothing new in the realm of therapy, especially marriage and family therapy. Our first sage in this realm, Ivan Boszormenyi-Nagy, is the father of contextual family therapy—the therapy of fairness and loyalty. A Hungarian immigrant to the United States, he came by his preoccupation with fairness and justice honestly: his father was a lawyer and a judge. Nagy famously said that contributing to the very survival of the planet was "therapy's ultimate mandate for humanity."[2] If we don't have this pale blue dot to stand on, it doesn't matter how we feel about it or each other. We're all connected, but how do we honor this connection? To put it another way: what do we owe to each other?[3] Our second sage, Carl Sagan, an American Jew and first-generation Ukrainian immigrant on his father's side of the genogram (or therapy family tree) might respond that we owe as much to the universe as it owes to us, as we are each part of the other. Sagan, the famed multihyphenate astronomer–planetaryscientist–cosmologist–astrophysicist–astrobiologist–author, spoke and wrote extensively on the interconnectedness of human beings and the cosmos.

After a day of hiking and mindful meditation at the pond, you've grown weary. The rest of the campers have split off onto different trails, and so, as dusk descends and night falls, you make camp in a glen. Over a simple meal of beans and carrots, you watch as the stars come out. Rather than pitching your tent, you decide to sleep outside in the cool night air under the starscape. You snuggle down into your soft sleeping bag, stretching out your feet and wiggling your toes. Yawning, you look up at the sky and notice that these constellations look quite different from the ones back home. Directly above you blinks what you decide are two distinct constellations. The first comprises seven stars in the vague shape of a falcon. To the falcon's right (your left) sits the second constellation in the round shape of a turtle. The stars you've designated as the eyes of each animal seem to wink at you. Deciding they're friendly, you smile at them as your eyelids become heavier.

When you wake, you are no longer outdoors, but rather in, and the scene is astonishing. You look around and realize that you're sitting at a desk in an interstellar therapy room made to accommodate the various sizes of celestial bodies. You look out the window and see the rings of Saturn and the dust storms of Mars. The sight is awe-inspiring and a bit overwhelming. To regain your composure, you redirect your attention to the room where you awoke. You move to explore your desk and notice that on the computer screen an appointment reminder is blinking. Your next client is ... Earth?

You look out the window again and watch as Earth slowly drifts into view. You marvel as her orbit shifts, realizing that Earth is, indeed, making her way toward you. Judging from the angle of her orbit and present velocity, you realize you have about fifteen minutes to prepare. How might you conceptualize Earth as a client? You sit and thoughtfully consider what you already know of Earth and all she has been through. Your client is aged and has experienced so much over her long life. She also has a large and disparate family that includes all of the many species who inhabit her. Earth is ill. She has had many stressors in her time, brought about by the system of which she is a part. First there was a major precipitating event that created the whole universe. Then, as with any system, the more beings that joined the system of Earth, the more complicated the system became. Each part trying to do what they believed to be best, but few asking Earth what she wanted. She has been screaming out like the scapegoat in the family system, begging to be acknowledged. Over the last several centuries, Earth's most tempestuous species has been creating both change and discord. The human species with all its many modern "advances" is abusing Earth, making the whole system stand up and take notice.

Before you begin this session with Earth, you may need some consultation. Who knows more about Earth than the constellations in her sky? You turn to your left and walk out onto the observation deck. There are those constellations again! The Falcon and the Turtle blink brightly at you as they explain that they've spent billions of years learning how best to understand and care for Earth and her family. They're in a position to offer expert guidance as your clinical team.

Falcon invites you to remember the importance of getting curious about fairness and equity. He asks you to consider how Earth might feel when she reviews the family ledger, a metaphorical book of debits and credits recording who owes what to whom.[4] Have the human beings of Earth's family treated her with the care and consideration she has shown them? Perhaps already you're sitting with the reality that Earth's family ledger is not balanced. Even though the goal is never complete equity in the ledger, the difference between the sides in Earth's ledger is so big that it's causing resentment. Falcon reminds you that although resentment can be a corrosive emotion leading to conflict and risking generational cutoff, you mustn't gloss over the validity of Earth's feelings. Her resentment, anger, and sadness have accumulated over many millennia.

You turn to Falcon's companion, Turtle, and ask for his thoughts and musings. Turtle wishes for you to remember that everything is connected: we are made of star stuff. And so whatever happens to Earth happens to her family, and vice versa. When we view Earth from far away, we witness that she is but a pale blue dot, with the family upon her infinitesimally small. Turtle reminds us of the importance of zooming in and out to notice that we are each infinite and infinitely small.

The constellation consult team reminds you they'll be observing your session through the one-way mirror, offering feedback during the midway point of this first therapy session with Earth. You glance up at the clock and realize it's time for your next session. Falcon gives you an affirmative wink and Turtle gives you a gentle blink before you leave the observation deck and your observation team takes their place behind the one-way mirror. You go to the doors of your office and they slide open with a gentle sigh to reveal Earth.

You begin the session as you would any other, by asking: "Earth, what brings you in today?" She shares her distress—feelings of sadness, anger, and despair over the death of her coral reefs, the rise and spread of viruses caused by family members crossing her boundaries, the melting of her ice caps, and the death of so many of her varied and vibrant flora and fauna.[5]

It probably comes as no surprise that we, the authors, take Earth's distress seriously. We don't conceptualize her cries for help as being reactionary or due to some planetary version of generalized anxiety disorder. Climate change is not a matter of opinion. It is an observable phenomenon. If this all feels new for you, reader, we invite you to embrace some of Carl Rogers's unconditional positive regard[6] for your client. It is her reality that she is struggling. It is her reality that she is in pain and that parts of her are dying. Our world's climate is changing, and that will alter the ways in which both we as human beings and all other life exists on this planet. And some forms of life will no longer exist. In fact, there are already some forms of life that no longer exist.

Sometimes clinicians avoid or sidestep issues of anxiety tied to climate collapse for fear that the topic is too political for the therapy space. If this sounds familiar to you, we, the authors, invite you to sit with the radical notion that everything is political. In this case, with Earth as our client, we cannot ignore what is in front of us. Her pain comes from the "political." Consider for a moment how you feel—not in the therapy space, but in your own life—around the game of politics. Although politics may feel separate from your life, the impact of politics profoundly impacts all of us on a daily basis. Access to clean water, availability of nutrient-dense food, the presence of food deserts, and even the shade provided by trees are all controlled by politics. For our client, Earth, her concerns are both personal and political, individual and communal. As you validate her feelings, you notice yourself becoming overwhelmed. Perhaps you're experiencing the feeling of sadness and despair that can come up when existential dread turns to a fear of clear and present danger.

This is an opportunity to reckon with your feelings, beliefs, and opinions around climate change and Earth's pain. You realize that now is the time to consult with your clinical team, constellations Falcon and Turtle. You invite Earth to engage in a mindfulness breathing exercise while you rejoin your consultants behind the one-way mirror.

The consultation team is compassionate. They can see how your clinical time with Earth distresses you. Falcon invites you to pause and reflect on both your personal and your familial experiences. Depending on where you live, how and where you were raised, your cultural and ethnic background, your gender expression, and your current social class, which is to say, your *intersectionality*, Falcon reminds that you will be differently impacted by climate collapse. Falcon invites you to consider that your awareness and emotional presence also matter, explaining: "Earth experiences climate collapse viscerally. But so much of modern life has focused on separating human beings from their inherent connectedness to Earth and all her creatures. Consider the sourcing of the food you eat, the clothes you wear, the material from which your home is built. How much choice and knowledge do you have when it comes to both attaining and maintaining these resources? Given the choices that you do have, what impact do these individual choices have on you and the animals, plants, and human communities connected to these resources?"[7]

You share with Falcon your current relationship to the planet and other species of life. You reflect on how resource distribution, legislation, and the fate of birth impact your experience of life. You consider how even something as simple as ownership of land eventually leads to the modern capitalist practice of resource hoarding. As Falcon names these thoughts with you, he normalizes your experience and helps you to understand how climate collapse is impacting you and the many communities to which you belong. You put a hand to your head to steady yourself. You must admit that you feel a bit dizzy as you consider the many ways that you affect and are impacted by the diverse forms of existence. Falcon advises you to take slow and steady breaths. When you're ready, you look up at the constellation team and blink your eyes.

Turtle reminds you that you are insignificant in the face of the cosmos. This shocks you, so you ask Turtle to please say more about that. He smiles and gently clarifies that your individual experience shapes your perspective; that is, you experience life through your singular self. Earth's perspective is inherently communal; she directly experiences the death of hundreds of species, the collapse of coral reefs, the burning of her forests, and the increasing number of unhoused humans. This suffering is not abstract for her. She is fully emotionally present in each of these disasters. Turtle invites you to consider how you might be both an individual and a community. You thank the consultants for these thoughts, though you feel like you have some stuff to talk about in your own therapy later.

You return to session with Earth with a renewed sense of compassion for her experience. You find that you're able to ask your countertransference to take a step back so you can be fully present with her, and you affirm that everything she is describing is pain. She has experienced and is now experiencing trauma. You let her know that you see and hear her and that you are here for her now. She is not alone.

Before the session closes, Earth invites you to join her in the outer space of the solar system, explaining: "It gives you a perspective unlike any other." First you'll need to put on your space suit. Walk to the closet where you keep your interstellar travel attire and select a space suit that optimizes oxygen. Now step into your suit, making sure everything is tight and secure. Once you lock your helmet into place, you're ready to join Earth in outer space. When you join her out among the stars, you do indeed feel flooded with thoughts and feelings you had never before considered. You and Earth float in space for several minutes. You thank her for this experience.

After you return to your office and put away your space suit, you lie back on your chaise longue and consider all you have experienced. After a time, you visit with your constellation friends. Falcon asks: "Can you form a therapeutic alliance with Earth?" Turtle asks: "Can you have compassion for Earth and respect her struggles?"

"Let's sleep on it," you reply.

In the morning you find yourself returned to camp with much to ponder. You take out your map and begin to draw.

Grieving Tools—The Town Crier

In these beleaguered times, we can feel compelled to constantly sound the alarm in person, on social media, and within ourselves; but if we're constantly performing the role of town crier, we risk emotional and physical burnout. We also run the risk of losing our ability to discern the difference between immediate danger and the emergent danger. This is all the more complicated in the context of climate collapse, when those in positions of power maintain the status quo while the United Nations keeps making it clear that our window for action is rapidly closing.[8] The receivers or listeners within many modern systems are not always the group members given the power to enact change.

Client

What do you tell your client to do when they experience environmental injustice? We invite you to welcome them to cry out in both a literal and a figurative sense. When we think of injustices, we think of a town where the status quo has long been established. It takes the town crier to shake up the system and tell it that the status is no longer quo. In the olden days, the town crier's job was to sound the literal alarm, which usually meant ringing a literal bell, to announce to the community that immediate action was needed: *Sven's barn is on fire! The bandits are attacking the village! Bears have gotten into the beehives!* The town crier performed the crucial function of rallying us all together to prevent total (or partial) annihilation.

As you and your clients continue to experience the impact of climate collapse, they can, and often do, experience pressure to constantly and consistently sound the alarm.

But even the person in the role of truth teller needs to pause and rest sometimes. This tool provides clinicians with concrete language to help clients begin to first notice and then start a dialogue with their own inner town crier.

In the therapy space, you can use the town crier label to first validate your client's assessment of a dire situation (if applicable) and then invite them to explore with you the question of whether the given situation calls for them to take on the burden of announcing the emergency. Much like the old tale of the boy who cried wolf, there is an important role for the town crier—it tells us when there is danger—but that part of us can't tell the difference between different types of danger. Is it a wolf, or Virginia Woolf? That is, is there danger, or is there a part of us that needs our attention and compassion? Town criers get tired, too. You can't stay alert all day every day watching for bandits without taking any time for a little self-care. So we invite you to work with your client to help them get to know their internal town crier and befriend it, so the two of them can decide together when they need to scream out loud for all to hear that there is danger in the town that must be stopped.

Therapist

This tool of the town crier can help you navigate your own personal struggles outside of session. The town crier metaphor invites you, the clinician, to notice when you're triggered in session by comments and beliefs that your clients express. As discussed in the Realm of Our Plague, it may not always be therapeutically appropriate to challenge your client's beliefs or opinions related to climate change. And yet for those of us who feel deeply invested in the state of our planet, it can feel monumentally difficult to let such an "opportunity" pass.

When you notice your inner town crier being activated in session, the first thing you can do is pause and notice this part of yourself. As you listen to your client (let's call her Ruby) complain about her sister who "spent all of Kwanzaa talking about micro-plastics and the ocean," you might find yourself aligning with Ruby's sister and wanting to join her in her town crying. What a useful piece of information! Whenever this sort of noticing pops up for us in session, it's an indication that we're experiencing *countertransference*. Countertransference is presented as being negative, but truly it's just information. Your own system is informing you that there's something in the content or affect of your client's presentation that feels resonant to you as a human person. Instead of pushing this awareness away and labeling it as "bad," we invite you to get curious about what's pulling at your attention. If you find that there's some unresolved work you need to do, ask your internal town crier to step back. But if your town crier is trying to tell you that there's a way to reach Ruby, you can decide to use this countertransference to engage with Ruby from a place of understanding and compassion that was *prompted* by your town crier but that does not *come from* your town crier. Town criers are excellent alarm systems, but they are not therapists, so take a moment to make sure you acknowledge your town crier, thank them for their service, and then come back to your therapist self before you address Ruby.

Outside the therapy space, you may want to use somatic techniques like progressive muscle relaxation to help integrate[9] and release the alarm bells that rang through your system when you were in session with Ruby, or when you read the updated report from the UN climate panel, or when a colleague casually mentions that "single-use plastic just makes life so much easier." Even if you decided it was appropriate to take the action that your inner town crier suggested, you likely still have adrenaline and other hormones moving through your system. Taking time to validate your town crier and to then "complete the stress response cycle,"[10] as advocated by famed burnout researchers Amelia and Emily Nagoski, helps ensure that you will be able to cry out to the town another day.

Due North: Self of the Therapist

As we think about ourselves as therapists, we look toward a sinking ship: the RMS *Titanic*, and not the James Cameron fanfiction. As a Titanic scholar, Justine has found the "unsinkable" ship to be a beautiful example of how intersectionality plays out in the real world as well as a useful framing device to get curious with ourselves about how we're spending our time on this planet—not just as therapists, but as people.

For the *Titanic*, as on our planet, there were early indicators that there were problems. By the time they decided to turn the wheel, it was too late. But in the two-hour period for which the ship was sinking, the passengers had a few choices. The crew knew they would go down with the ship. It was the duty they had signed on for. Some passengers didn't believe that the unsinkable ship would indeed sink, and they went about their evening right up until the final inevitable moments when they were shocked to discover they were dying. Others, particularly those in third class, tried desperately to get to a position in which they could survive.[11] These stories are all heartbreaking; most resonant for us, though, is the story of the Titanic band.

These musicians, knowing that the ship was indeed sinking and that they would not get a seat in any of the lifeboats, did what they did best: they played. They stood on the deck and they played their instruments together. Some historians believe this was to calm the passengers,[12] and we don't disagree. But we also believe there was another motivation. The band members had two hours to live, and when given the option to decide how they wanted to spend that time, they all decided: "doing what I love." They spent those final hours making meaning in the best way they knew how—making music together. Their playing had the ripple effect of calming others, and survivors spoke of it for the rest of their lives: "Many brave things were done that night, but none more brave than by those few men playing."[13] "They played until the ship was lost and finally the band leader said 'gentlemen, thank you all. A commendable performance. Good night, and good luck.'"[14]

As therapists, our role is sometimes to provide comfort and support to our clients in the same way that the band provided comfort and support to the passengers on the RMS *Titanic*. But sometimes we find that we're racing to get in a lifeboat, leaving other passengers stranded. Perhaps you're struggling with feelings of nihilism around making any changes in your life: *Why should I even try to feel better or work on anything if the ship is going down anyway?* We understand this feeling, and we invite you to get curious with yourself about this question: who do you want to be?

We reject the toxic positivity narratives claiming that you can "manifest" anything you want, and we instead invite you to consider what you would do with your final two hours. Do you consider yourself someone who has made a vow to serve and will help others into the lifeboats, no matter what happens to you? Will you hold your loved ones close as the waters rise? Will you play music until the last possible note? Will you seek safety for yourself and those around you?

Unlike the sinking of the *Titanic*, it will take years to suffer through the pain and struggles of climate collapse. If you have already read chapter 1, it might be beneficial to recall the tool from that realm: the neutral zone. Take a moment to notice your roles on the good ship planet Earth.

Due West: Supervision

If you're a supervisee and you aren't sure how your supervisor would feel about bringing global and social justice topics into your supervision relationship, consider simply acknowledging this reality. You can ask your supervisor what their stance is on bringing collective trauma topics into the supervision relationship. If your supervisor doesn't answer in the affirmative, ask if they would be open to discussing it, because it's important to you. If your supervisor is unwilling to discuss important topics such as these with you, it might be an indication that this isn't the supervisor for you, and that's okay. Not all clinicians see the importance of this sort of meta-analysis, and it's not your job, supervisee, to convert them. You can thank this supervisor for their time and move along. That is, of course, if you have a supervisor whom you chose outside your agency. If this is your site supervisor, then you might want to consider adding supervision outside your agency with a clinician who more fully embodies your values.

If you're a supervisor, there's no time like the present to contextualize how you manage climate distress within the supervision space. Many of you may already be thinking of instances when this came up within supervision. In our own work as supervisors, we often find that supervisees benefit from us taking the lead in naming the distress and the dread. Even when the present moment seems full to the brim with climate news, we have found that supervisees diligently avoid the crying planet in the room, preferring instead to talk about "that very difficult clinical case." This isn't their fault, of course. It's rare in therapy school to discuss which topics are acceptable to bring up both in supervision and in the therapy room. And many supervisors are uncomfortable bringing global struggles and social-justice topics to the couch or the supervision room. This is an opportunity both for supervisees to learn to talk about these systemic concerns and for supervisors to model that this is not only acceptable; it's mandatory.

As supervisors, it's our role to take the lead in naming and acknowledging, in this instance, climate dread and then asking the supervisee how they would like to proceed. Checking for consent and energy levels are both important considerations here. You, reader, made an informed choice when picking up this book. If you were uncertain about the book after reading just the title, certainly by the end of the introduction you understood what you were signing up for: this book takes an honest look at the tragedies that face us both inside and outside the therapy room. There was enough information in the beginning pages of the book for you to make an informed choice about whether to continue reading it. When working with a supervisee, part of what we want to model is taking the time to notice our own clinical energy levels so we can use this information to be effective clinicians.

Larisa has had supervision sessions where, upon asking a supervisee for consent to discuss climate topics, they have replied, "I do not have the energy to sit with climate collapse today. I have five therapy sessions after our meeting." In these scenarios, Larisa affirms and validates the supervisee's informed decision making and invites them to consider what they need from supervision this day. She'll say, "If we just need to focus on the clinical pieces, we can do that." Especially in those instances when the supervisee says they can't directly engage with climate collapse at this time, they're practicing the skill of acknowledging climate collapse. In both therapy and supervision, there is power in the simple act of naming or acknowledging a hard truth without moving to the second step of exploring calls to action about what has been named.

This is not the first time that clinicians have faced global catastrophe. It's not even the first time we've faced a national catastrophe. BIPOC clinicians have been navigating the struggle of therapising in an oppressive system for generations. If you're a BIPOC reader, then you're no stranger to asking for the support you need and finding that it's lacking—that your teachers and guides and sages don't understand and don't offer you what you need. You get to be discerning about and protective of your space, energy, and time. If supervisors and teachers whose role it is to help and support you aren't doing so, then you get to put your guard up until they show you they are safe. The world is dying. There is no more time for posturing and standing on ceremony. If the people in charge won't get over themselves enough to realize that they can't work the way they have in the past, then the dying world will pass them by.

Finding grieving allies is an important part of the grieving process. This might look like peer-to-peer consultation, or it might just be having a friend and colleague with whom you can freely share your grief. Being a therapist is hard work. We hold not only our own feelings but the feelings of our clients, and then we must simultaneously engage our skills, training, and powers of analysis to provide help and support—but not too much help and support, lest we do for clients what they must learn to do for themselves. It's crucial to have a community to whom you can turn for support as you grapple with the loss of the safe and healthy world we all wanted to practice in.

Due East: Education

Students, while you have indeed chosen a difficult time to start your journey, you have never been more needed. It can be difficult to learn everything you need to know about being a therapist on top of your own struggles in the world; not to mention your realization that all of the world's struggles wind up in the therapy room. We applaud you for wanting to be a part of this process. We're proud to pass the candle to you. Because you're entering the field in a volatile time in the world's history, we invite you to find that neutral zone of acknowledging, with or without acceptance. You are worth the time and energy it takes to take care of yourself in the midst of all of this, and you deserve teachers who will support you on your journey. If you feel you aren't receiving that, tell someone. The wheel can't be broken without those willing to stand up and demand that it be broken. You are the future, and the future is bright.

Perhaps you are fortunate enough to be in a graduate-level master's or doctoral program where the collective traumas of our world are being named and discussed, with consent, and with attention being paid to energy and compassion levels. To be honest, we, the authors, had a more complicated experience in graduate school, where we found the old systemic axiom "take what works and leave the rest" to be incredibly impactful, helpful, and appropriate. Justine and Larisa found that in their graduate program no time was given to talking about systemic concerns related to collective trauma. While much attention was given to historical and transgenerational traumas, professors did not spend time with the current global ills that face the living generations.

So much is asked of students, and it's certainly not our intention to task you with more. Our invitation to you is to first and foremost recognize that you deserve training and support around these present collective traumas. You deserve a safe space where you can be emotionally messy as a part of your training. We don't want you to carry more than your fair share, but unfortunately those who came before you in this world have made it so that you simply will be doing that. The earth as we know it is dying, and it's dying while you're at the helm of the therapy ship. This is a big responsibility, and we hope you know that there are those who see you, recognize your struggle, and thank you for your service. You'll be dealing with everything we discuss in this book for the rest of your careers. To pretend otherwise is disingenuous. We don't say this to be Debbie Downers; we say it to verbalize to normalize.

Teachers, please bring the outside in. You're teaching the next generation of clinicians, who are serving in an entirely different world from the one in which you learned to serve. What we recommend is likely uncomfortable and goes against all the rules we learned about being a tabula rasa for clients and students, but please allow yourselves to be fully human. Invite your students to also be fully human. Therapy school is not simply learning a bunch of facts to regurgitate on exams; it's learning how to be a healer. Many of us come to the profession because we have this innate skill, but we don't know how to place it in the context of also needing healing and living on a wounded Earth, or how to set our own boundaries. Teachers, you have a great power and a great responsibility.

Although we recognize that this can feel daunting, we want to highlight the depth and complexity this adds to the academic experience. While it is a big ask, it is also an unparalleled opportunity to offer Earth the future clinicians she so desperately needs and deserves.

South: Death and Love

As we near the end of the Realm of Our Earth, we invite you to return to your map. As you review your notes and drawings, think back to the final minutes of your session with Earth, when you joined her in outer space. While you hovered beside planet Earth, you started to notice the vastness of space. Perhaps a bit of vertigo set in and you momentarily lost control of your jet pack, spinning out and away from her orbit. But then you took a deep breath and pulled out of the spin. You returned to floating beside this great planet—the only Earth we will ever have. You began to realize: Earth is what floats between you and total oblivion. The human beings of early civilization often perceived the natural word as dangerous—an entity to be fought or bargained with, but rarely to collaborate with. We were a young species then. We can be wiser now.

Out here, floating in space, certain realities are more evident. Without Earth, there is only death. With Earth there is the possibility for so much growth and change and life. Many of the early human societies, such as early Central and South American cultures and Bronze Age tribes in Eastern Europe, worshiped the planet as a Goddess.[15] The natural world that encompassed both cruelty and joy was seen as a maternal figure for whom death was only part of a cyclical, regenerative cycle. We suggest that humanity's present perspective of planet-as-object or planet-as-adversary limits our ability to be present with ourselves and all life on this planet. What if we chose collaboration? What if we chose collective growth and healing that prioritizes the sanctity and value of all life, including the life of our home planet? Out here in space, the answer is clear: we're all we've got.

4

THE REALM OF OUR ORIGINS

> *"What makes us change?"* he asked again. *"Not an education—otherwise all educated people would be integrated and mature. Is it support? No, that's an illusion you get used to, like having a mother who always cooks for you. It's infantilizing."* And then, a third time: *"What really makes us change? Interaction between the therapist and family—radiation."*
> —CARL WHITAKER[1]

As you are now well aware, Justine and Larisa are marriage and family therapists. One of Justine's favorite theorists is American psychiatrist and marriage and family therapist Carl Whitaker. One of the founders of experiential family therapy, Carl believed that the best thing a therapist could do was shake up the family system. For him, that could look like throwing a frisbee at a client, making jokes at their expense, or passing out foam bats and encouraging family members to use them to duel each other.[2] Justine has lovingly nicknamed Carl the honey badger of marriage and family therapy.

It helps her students remember him! So who better to guide us through the land of our kin than that wily honey badger of marriage and family therapy, Carl Whitaker?

As Carl once said, you can't divorce your family.[3] You may notice yourself having a reaction to this quote. Rather than pushing away these feelings, memories, or thoughts, we invite you to make space for them. Family is a fraught experience, and even when we have the most detailed of maps, we can quickly end up in the swamp of sadness. While you can be assured that we aren't going to throw a frisbee at you, we are going to invite the shaking up of systems.

You have left the dangerous beauty of space and have traveled to the vast tundra of the Realm of Our Origins. After such a long journey, you need rest and refreshment. You pause and lean away from the wind, staring out over the frozen snowscape. After a few moments, you notice a brown blur moving in the distance. You blink and shake your head, wondering if mirages are as common in tundras as in deserts. But when you look up again, you see that the shape is indeed a form that is moving ever closer to you. Your muscles tense as you tighten the straps of your rucksack. Ready for anything, you bend slightly at the knees as the stranger crests a snow hill, and you realize: it's a honey badger! What is it doing in the tundra? Before you can even begin to answer this question, the badger is upon you, chittering and shaking its body to and fro.

He seems quite friendly, actually, and after gently patting your left knee with his paw, he seems to motion you onward in a direction north by northwest. You follow Honey Badger for several meters before you notice a faint light in the distance. After several more meters, you can distinguish the faint outline of a lodge. You stop and stare in wonderment. The lodge has two large, well-lit windows in its face, and you begin to hope it will be a cozy spot to rest for the evening. Honey Badger beckons, and you follow him through the snow, chuckling at his quips.

Upon first entering the lodge, you kick off your snow boots and wrap yourself in a faux fur blanket. You take a seat next to a crackling fireplace, noticing that a small table has been set with cups, saucers, and both cocoa and tea fixings. You take a warm mug of cocoa and offer a steaming cup of tea to Badger. The heat from the mug begins to spread from the tips of your fingers up through your forearms as the logs of the fire pop and hiss. You settle in with your snuggly accoutrements and your happy Honey Badger, and you start to turn inward.

Your Internal Family

What do you notice happening inside of yourself in this moment? Perhaps a part of you just hopped up and said, "I don't want to do that. Let's keep looking at the fire!" What you're experiencing is your *Internal Family Systems* (IFS). For the uninitiated, IFS is a therapeutic modality based on the concept of a multiplicity of the mind.[4] The core idea is that humans do not have one unitary mind; rather, we are made up of many different conscious *parts*, and a core or central *Self*. [5] If this does not immediately make sense, think about an orchestra. There are many different instruments that are all important and valid. That said, we cannot have a performance that is all tuba; that would be a lot of tuba. We can love the tuba and still acknowledge that it needs to take a step back so the other players get a chance to shine. Who decides this? The conductor (i.e., the Self) must be the one to guide when and how much the tuba plays. If the tuba becomes overwhelming, it is the conductor who must pull the tuba aside and have a chat about what is happening so they can get the orchestra back to playing in harmony.

The conductor might ask: "Hey, Tuba, why so much?"

And Tuba might stand up, careful not to knock over the stand holding their sheet music, and say: "I want to be heard!"

At which point the other members of the orchestra might begin to chatter, offering comments like: "But who *doesn't* hear you, Tuba?"

"But that's just the problem!" answers Tuba, stomping their foot. "Everyone *hears* me, but no one is *listening* to me!"

The conductor nods. "So you just play louder and louder because you want your sound to be heard and appreciated."

"Yes, that's right," Tuba says. "I know the other instruments have beautiful melodies. But I have a purpose in the orchestra, too."

"That makes sense, Tuba. Thank you for sharing that with me. I didn't realize that's what was happening for you, and now that I know, I'll be more attentive to your needs."

What you just witnessed, reader, is what IFS calls "parts work." The part—Tuba—can be seen and heard by all the other instruments (parts), but it is the engagement with Self (the conductor) that allows the part to feel seen and understood rather than judged. We mention this at the beginning of the chapter because we'll be using the framing of parts work throughout this realm. We've found IFS to be particularly helpful when holding space for families, both the external and internal kinds.

Now, let us return to the lodge. As you look around this metaphorical setting within your internal world, you might start to notice different personalities or parts. If you're Jungian in your therapeutic orientation, you might think of them as subpersonalities. If you're a narrative therapist or a play therapist, you might notice these parts as characters from play or fiction. However you experience these internal parts of you, we invite you to get curious with them about their feelings related to the topic of this chapter: the family or kinship groups of origin in all their many forms. Parts can exist outside therapeutic modality; we offer the IFS framing as simply one option.[6]

Family is complicated. No matter how much we or our family members want to ignore or bury the influence of family on the people we are now, there is no denying that we got how we got because of them. Even though we may change immensely as we grow, our lives are also informed by the folks who raised us—as are our very genes.[7] Genetics and environment have a far more complex relationship than was once thought. Biological ancestors self-evidently impact our genetic makeup, but the folks who raise us, regardless of their genetic connection to us, affect the way our genes express themselves.

In adulthood, there is often a tension between the desire to connect and the need to separate. Bowenians will recognize this process as *differentiation,* [8] the method by which people find ways to be both separate from and still connected to their family of origin. Differentiation is messy and can last for years or even a lifetime. You might have a few parts right now that are upset about this discussion of family and differentiation. They might say, "I hate our family!" or "Don't say negative stuff about the family!" or "Have we even thought about differentiation?!" Welcome, parts, we've been expecting you. Now take a deep breath and find that small spark of the most grounded Self energy that is possible for you right now. Then, we invite you to notice the parts of your personality that are present. Parts can be different ages, shapes, and colors, to name just a few possibilities. Parts can correspond to certain periods of your life, and they can also look or sound like folks you know or knew in the external world.[9] The mind is infinite, so your parts may look or sound very different from someone else's. Your inner world is uniquely your own. We invite you not to judge what you find there.

Once you've acknowledged each part, you might begin to get curious with them about who would like to stay for this discussion in the lodge and who would prefer to take a break. While this might be confusing for those who are still learning about IFS, we invite you to think about it from this perspective: at the end of a long day of therapising, do you continue to practice therapy while you move through the rest of your evening? Are you psychoanalyzing your partner while preparing the salad? It's quite common for therapists to need transition time between work and home; the need for this transition time is due to parts. The parts of you that hold your clinical training need transition time to check in with the Self and then take a break so that the parts of you that know how to engage with your best friend, roommate, or partner can step forward for their solo. Much like when the day shift is preparing to leave and the night shift arrives, there is some crossover where folks aren't quite sure who still needs to be there and what work needs to get done. How often do we blame the day shift for leaving something undone? Put another way, do you ever think to yourself, "Ugh, past-me, why didn't you do the laundry? Now I have no pants."

Now that you have a clearer understanding of what we mean by "asking parts to take a break," we invite you to take a few moments and determine which parts need to be here for this conversation and which parts don't. Some parts might be too young to understand what's going on, and this might be scary for them. We invite you to see where else these parts might want to stay while you're reading this chapter. Some of our favorite locations are the beach and "the breakroom of our minds," but any place they want to be is fine. Take a moment and let those parts go there and then come back. Be sure to tell them you'll check in with them later.

Generational Dissonance

In the spirit of Carl Whitaker, we're going to shake up the system yet again by inviting in another therapy guide. Let's welcome Pauline Boss, the patron saint of ambiguous loss, to our lodge. She'll have tea, thanks. A marriage and family therapist with deep familial roots in the Midwestern Swiss-American community, Pauline has much to share about the complicated nature of ambiguous loss and ambivalence. Originally, Pauline conceived of ambiguous loss as any loss that wasn't clear-cut, such as the disappearance of a loved one, relocating, relationship breakups, and job loss.[10] Now Pauline theorizes that there is ambiguity in all losses, even those that are quite straightforward, such as a loved one dying.[11]

Today we've invited Pauline over to share her thoughts about the divide between family members and family generations as it relates to our most recent national and global losses due to the pandemic and political unrest, including the attack on the US Capitol on January 6, 2021: "While we were more divided than since the Civil War, with conflict in families and a mob storming our nation's capital, we learned about absurdity and paradox. Presence and absence, facts and fiction, were muddled. Even a leader was ambiguously lost, missing in Action."[12]

Let us pause and notice how each of our present parts reacted to this quote. You might notice that some of them immediately spoke up in disagreement, saying something like, "There's no need to be reactionary, Pauline." Or perhaps they responded with a more logic-based argument: "Well, I think we can all agree that history is full of examples of generational conflict. Ours just seems special because we are right here in it." Perhaps still other parts responded with the succinct, "Shut up, Pauline." It is also possible that many or all of your parts simply agreed with her statement. Perhaps they found affirmation and validation in her so bluntly naming what feels so true. As is usual with IFS, we offer the gentle reminder that all "parts are welcome."[13]

Pauline's most recent work speaks directly to current discord between family generations. Many of you may be familiar with the term *cognitive dissonance*, which describes the emotional state of holding simultaneous awareness of at least two feelings or thoughts that are in conflict with one another.[14] Many of us, the authors very much included, find ourselves navigating cross-generational relationships with adult family members who experience reality in radically different ways from us. Being in direct contact with them can feel like sharing space with someone who denies the existence of gravity, and their experience of you likely feels just as confounding to them. To quote one of our family members who is two generations older: "Everything I thought was real, you say doesn't exist anymore." This particular family member shared this in the context of a conversation about gender, and admittedly, this was hard to hear; but upon further reflection, the common ground became clearer. Although each generation understands the details or the content of the dissonance differently, both sides are experiencing and grappling with its impact.

Our family shapes who we are and who we continue to be, and we have to decide how to interact with them—or not—for our own well-being. They remain with you because they're already a part of you. They might even be one of the parts speaking to you right now.

If you're noticing a part or parts that resemble or embody one or more of your family members, we invite you to pause before reading further in this chapter. You might want to set the book aside and take some time with these family parts or the feelings and memories evoked by their presence. Remember what Carl Whitaker said: "You can never get divorced."[15] While that's true, we gently remind Carl that you can certainly take internal or external breaks from the people with whom you're connected.

In recent years, social media has been aflutter with videos and infographics about cutting toxic people out of your life. Although we don't want to come down on the side of keeping toxic people in your life, we do want to say there's no way to actually cut people out, because the ghost of our loved ones will remain with us in the form of parts. Thus, even if we cut someone out of our lives for safety—which makes sense—we still must heal that part that holds the loved one's memory and the parts that were hurt by them. Cutoff is a beginning, not an ending. As one of the characters in our favorite fandom, *Supernatural,* once observed: "Nothing ever really ends ... does it?"[16]

As you consider working with your clients and their difficult relationships with family of origin, we invite you to remember that when you're working with the client, their family is in the room with you whether they're physically present or not, because they're inside your client. If you're a clinician who has historically only worked with individuals or who sees people through a lens of individual autonomy, this is an opportunity to question that construct. Allow the parts that have feelings about it to come out and voice them.

Perhaps you've already guessed where we're going with this: if your client's family and community members are in the therapy room with you, then aren't your own family and community members present in the room as well? Yes, the multiverse is always present. At this moment, Pauline looks up from her tea and invites you to consider both/and thinking. Both/and thinking is a touchstone of systemic therapy that offers resolution when synthesis is impossible. But what do you do when your client is expressing pain over a recent argument with their mother, who is an avowed adherent of QAnon (more on QAnon in chapter 6), and this brings up your own memories of similar arguments with your Uncle Moishe at Seder? Perhaps in this example both/and thinking helps you find compassion for Uncle Moishe who is living in terror of COVID-19 even as he refuses to take what you feel are necessary safety steps, like getting vaccinated or wearing a mask when using public transportation. Both/and thinking may also be helpful to your client. But what if you have not yet found this compassion for Uncle Moishe? If you have yet to find healing or at least neutrality with your own family members, then your client's familial struggles will only mean that you have more rankled and cantankerous family members with whom to deal.

Grieving Tool: Return to Sender

Enmeshment is the emotional equivalent of one human coercing another to share a major organ with them. Enmeshment is the shadow side of empathy, and even clinicians can be susceptible to the emotional confusion it provokes. Is this feeling mine, or does it belong to Uncle Moishe? Why am I still feeling sad? Is it because my last three clients of the day expressed sadness, or is this sadness my own? The return-to-sender tool invites you to pinpoint the physical and emotional signs that a feeling you are experiencing is not, in fact, your own and it then invites you to pass that emotion back to its rightful owner. In session, you can teach the return-to-sender tool to your clients to help them work through painful family enmeshment. This can also be a helpful and compassionate way to return the feelings you received from a particular client back to them. While we as therapists do hold space for our clients' feelings, we must not be confused for the keeper of these feelings.

Client

Emotional attunement with our clients can be an incredibly helpful skill. However, holding emotions for our clients instead of helping them learn to identify and manage their own feelings is not just counterproductive; it's harmful to both you and your client. If you notice feelings of extreme overwhelm, the physical sensation of heaviness following a session, or emotional confusion, then you may be holding your client's feelings long after the session has ended. In those cases, we must hand back what they've given us. They gave it to us in good faith because they trust us, so we honor that trust by letting them know "actually, this isn't mine" and emotionally returning their feelings to them. You might want to visualize yourself literally writing or stamping "return to sender" on the emotional letter that was sent to you. This is not unkind. In fact, when a letter goes to the wrong place, the kindest thing to do is to return it where it came from so it can get to the person who truly needs the message.

Justine has experienced clients sending her urgent text messages to request "emergency" sessions during her off hours. During her preclinical years, when this would happen Justine would become emotionally charged, heart pounding, and feel the need to respond to these requests immediately—even in the middle of the night. During a supervision talk, Justine's supervisor reminded her that she's not a crisis service. These clients were desperately trying to give their overwhelming feelings to Justine to hold for them, and Justine was receiving those feelings with open arms, holding them until the next session. This conversation with her supervisor allowed Justine to reconceptualize the "emergency" text. She considered it an invitation for her attention. When something like that happens now, she responds with an inquiry about the nature of the issue and asks what the client has already tried. Does the client require a crisis line? Or do they simply not want to sit with their feelings? Depending on the answer, Justine will decide how to respond to the invitation. Often the response is: "Practice your skills, and we will meet soon."

Therapist

The gifts that brought us to the therapy field do not cease to exist with our last session of the day. Skills like emotional attunement, empathy, analysis, and compassion remain with us as we move through our days. However, we need to bring attention to how these therapy parts show up for us in our daily lives outside of session, lest we find ourselves compassionately consoling our doctor following their recent divorce during our own annual physical. The return-to-sender tool can help us in our daily lives whenever we notice that we're either engaging our therapist parts outside the office or simply noticing that a person close to us is having a big feeling.

Once, while Larisa was on a break in her local park, she encountered a very stressed mother and child. The mother parked her car right next to Larisa despite there being ample space in the lot, rolled down her window, and proceeded to talk to Larisa as if the two had just started a session. Keep in mind that Larisa had never met this person before and was off duty between in-home family therapy appointments. At that moment, Larisa had a choice: she could roll down her own window and begin a dialogue with a fellow human traveler, or she could mark this envelope full to bursting with emotion, and return to sender. In that instance, Larisa returned this stranger's feelings back to them by rolling up her window, reclining her seat, and closing her eyes.

Due North: Self of the Therapist

Sitting with all the different parts of you is both terrifying and profoundly liberating. Realizing how much of your family system is alive and (not necessarily) well inside of you can be scary. Justine had this experience in her first IFS training. She discovered a part that was holding something deep and unexpected from her family system, and being able to unburden that part opened up new possibilities for her. After assuring herself that she had not joined a cult (a fear one of her parts still has even after many years of study), she got curious with one of the training assistants about how this part could be there. Justine exclaimed, "I've been in my own therapy for over a decade!"

The assistant replied, "A part of you has." This response was maddening.

This realization also brought up significant ambiguous loss for Justine. She experienced mourning around the years of therapy where these parts had felt unheard, and she felt anger that other clinicians had not brought the message of these parts to her conscious awareness. This realization also brought forward a horrible thought—that she had more healing to do. And at the same time, she experienced a great awakening to entirely new questions and possibilities about her own healing as well as that of her clients. When this realization entered the scene, she became profoundly sad, realizing she could never use this revelation to help her navigate her relationships with her parents, who were both gone by this time. And yet there was a new and more resonant narrative she could use in discussing ideas like countertransference: *Which part of me is being activated by a part of them?* When she noticed that a part was "up," she knew she wasn't meeting her client from Self energy.

We recognize that not everyone is excited about doing hundreds of hours of IFS trainings, and that's okay. You don't have to. We merely invite you to notice what's happening in your own family system, both externally and internally. And if this information doesn't resonate for you as it does for us, that's okay, too. Take what works for you, and leave the rest.

Due West: Supervision

Talking about the family system is a vital part of the supervisory process. We, the authors, believe that thinking systemically is the best way to understand any individual human. No human lives in a vacuum—not even therapists. In fact, therapists least of all. Supervisees, you're constantly bombarded with reminders of your own family system, and you're being asked to hold space for aspects of it that may be difficult for you. Countertransference gets a bad rap in the therapy industry, but it's simply the awareness that a part of you has been activated by a part of the client. What great information to have! Supervisees often feel they need to hide their authentic humanness from their supervisors or else they'll be seen as weak or not doing their job properly. We all come from a family of origin. There is an infinitude of different ways this can look, and they can all be triggered by the right client in the right circumstance. You're not alone, and if you bring this to your supervisor, you might even be able to find some healing early in your career.

Supervisors, we offer a reminder that it is okay to be people. We can hold ethical boundaries and still make meaningful disclosures that can have a healing impact for our supervisees. Supervisees need to know that we are people and clinicians who have grown and changed and did not always have the answers. We do not become "less than" by sharing our experience; if anything, it teaches our supervisees that it's okay to make mistakes and to experience countertransference. Early in her supervisory training, Larisa worried about the potential risks of supervisor self-disclosure. After a parentified childhood and a series of complicated relationships when she was a supervisee, she wanted to avoid overburdening her supervisees at all costs. During a consultation conversation, Larisa asked Justine, "What if I cry? What if I overemote?" Justine replied: "You mean you haven't cried already?"

Although this question wasn't worded as sensitively as it could have been, it did help Larisa remember that she is fundamentally an emotional being whose primary mode of emotional expression is through her tears. To hide this part of herself from her supervisees would amount to hiding herself and perpetuating the false dichotomy between professional and human being. Justine pointed out that Larisa had the opportunity to normalize grieving in the supervisor-supervisee dyad because Larisa is an emotional being. Justine also offered the helpful reminder that if Larisa became emotional while effectively managing her own emotions, that would be beneficial social modeling.

After much reflection and consultation, Larisa invited her sadness into her supervisory space. Initially, Larisa found this uncomfortable and exhausting, but in time she found it to be a relief. When closing with one of her first supervisees after two years of work together, the supervisee shared that one of the most impactful parts of the supervision had been when Larisa cried: "I think about what you said to me that day all the time. That our clients don't need us to be perfect. They need us to be human."

Due East: Education

Students, you might find family-of-origin work to be particularly challenging and present for you because of the time in history when you're becoming a therapist. All therapists must reckon with the family they were born into, but many are able to find an equilibrium. For this generation of therapists, there is a climate of such divisiveness in families that it presents a significant challenge. This division will likely seep into your studies and your future work.

Recently Justine has spoken with students about how to work with folks who hold vastly different opinions from your own. Students are afraid of seeing their own families reflected back at them through their future clients. When students express these fears, Justine responds: "I invite you to offer compassion to yourself as much as you offer it to your clients. Remember that all of our behavior comes from our own thoughts, feelings, and experiences. You will start to notice your own parts and get to know them so that they can be friends to you in school and the therapy room to let you know that they need support. You will do your best."

Teachers, you have a tough new road ahead of you. The landscape of the family has changed, and therefore, so has your work as educators. Students now need a much better grasp of family dynamics, whether they're MFT-bound or not. It's vital for students to have a sense of their own family-of-origin work and legacies, as these will carry forward into their preclinical life and beyond. Teachers, we know you are underpaid and overworked, and we appreciate all that you do to give the next generation of therapists the best chance of staying in the field and thriving. We also invite you to spend time with your own internal system. This is difficult work, and it's worth it to get to know the family that lives inside of you. While it takes effort, the reward is greater emotional space in which to show up for your students.

Due South: Death and Love

Night has fallen in the mountains. As you look out the window, you see that snow is falling downward. A crescent moon hangs in the sky. You look back toward the fire and see that Honey Badger is asleep on the rug, his head pillowed on his crossed forepaws. Perhaps unsurprisingly, you see that Pauline Boss is still awake, making notes in a double-wide journal. She has one final support to offer us: the meaning-making of ambiguous loss. As you prepare to take your leave of this realm, you might make some space for arguably the most fraught experience of this realm: the death or loss of a family member.

While so much of our individual and collective existence is predicated on the importance of practice and multiple opportunities to learn a skill, you only get one shot at death. What we mean to suggest is that perhaps part of our collective human fear of death is due to its singular nature. You will only ever die once. And your parents—as well as your grandparents, siblings, aunts, uncles, cousins—will only ever die once. How do you craft an ending that is both meaningful and healing? One that honors the complicated nature of your human relationship? How might you transfer this knowledge or experience to your work as a therapist? If you notice part or all of you becoming overwhelmed by the enormity of these questions, we invite you to take a moment. You might even return to the winter scene or the cozy fire in the lodge. Pauline has some helpful perspectives when you feel ready.

Although you only ever experience the literal death of a family member once, you will have the rest of your life to understand this death and to learn ways to grieve. For those who had a neutral or positive relationship with the kin who raised them, it might be comforting to recall what we learned about Internal Family Systems earlier in this chapter: the kin who raised us are always within us, a part of our personality and our being-in-the-world. So even though the death of a family member is the end of your external relationship, your internal relating will continue.

For those of us with more complicated feelings toward the kin who raised us, we may feel ambivalent at best and angry at worst when faced with the idea that even death is not the end of our challenging relationship with such kin. Of course, our feelings about the folks who raised us change over time as we realize more about our own internal landscapes. Family therapists know that situations like estrangement or total cutoff from family of origin do not resolve or end the intergenerational hurt. Physical space can allow for physical and emotional safety while kinship members learn how to care for their own internal systems. For most, part of this journey involves ambiguous grieving for the kind of family that they desperately needed as a child but simply did not have. Sometimes this grief helps you find new ways to accept your family of origin as they are or were. Perhaps you recognize that members of your family of origin did the best they could, but the best they could was not nearly enough; nor was it what you needed. Pauline reminds us that the journey of ambiguous grief is perilous and unique. Death of kin both does and does not change this ambiguity. As a therapist, the more you're able to honor the finiteness of death and the infiniteness of grief, the more you'll be able to hold compassionate space for your clients.

Did you think we would forget Honey Badger? Or perhaps you envisioned him sleeping all the way through these steps in the Realm of Our Grief. Well, Carl Whitaker, ever the mercurial sage, has some final tools to offer before he beds back down for the night. You might imagine a human Carl standing at a podium delivering the following bit of advice; or, if you're in a sillier frame of mind, you might imagine him doling out wisdom on the hearth rug as he graciously accepts a cup of tea and plate of crumpets from his friend Pauline (she actually was one of his mentees in graduate school). Regardless of how you imagine him, Carl would be remiss if he did not remind us that what you don't pass back, you pass forward. In typical Carl fashion, there is love hidden in this riddle. The cherished memories you hold, the beloved lessons you learned, the turns of phrase, even the facial expressions you experienced with your loved ones remain with you.

Of course, this principle applies to everything you experience in your family of origin. This is why Carl reminds us that you don't have to keep everything your family gives you. For example, if you came from a family that practiced bottling up their anger until they exploded and broke things, you can pass that behavior back. If in this same family there was an emphasis placed on reading and a love of books, and these practices resonate with you, you can keep these practices. You can keep the aspects of your internal family that you love, while releasing or passing back those aspects or practices that do not serve you.

5
THE REALM OF OUR KIN

There are aspects of our inner or relational lives that we avoid being in touch with because we cannot tolerate what we feel when we touch the memories or emotions attached to them.... Yet these discomforting facets of ourselves are treasures of human experience that bond us to the rest of humanity.
—HARRY APONTE[1]

In this realm we explore the loves we choose. They may be platonic or romantic or a hybrid concoction. They may involve humans, pets, or plants that become family. We, the authors, do not consider the romantic relationship to be the center of emotional life, as many societal norms suggest. Rather, we believe that it's the families or communities we choose, in all their varied forms, around which we center our narratives.

Our guide in the Realm of Our Kin is Dr. Harry Aponte, a self-described "New York Puerto Rican" therapist who entered the nascent field of marriage and family therapy in 1961. In the late 1960s and early '70s Harry helped his colleagues and the future founders of structural family therapy, like Sal Minuchin, by introducing the then-radical concept of not just considering but directly involving the community in the family's healing journey. Harry linked his skills with community as a direct result of his childhood experiences: "It's not that they [Sal Minuchin, Virginia Satir, and Murray Bowen] ignored it, it's that I lived it. I grew up in it."[2]

When Harry was coming up in the field, most family therapists were still firmly rooted in Freudian psychoanalysis and the therapist-as-surgeon model. Harry, in contrast, leaned into his cultural heritage and his own humanness to connect with his clients and the communities in which he served.[3] Instead of being an authority or a dispassionate technician, he became part of the neighborhood in which his clients lived, eventually creating a training model that centered the human or person of the therapist[4] as the focal point of healing in the client-therapist and supervisor-supervisee relationship: "We're talking about a transformation. We're talking about something that is revolutionary.... Creating something and training a person who says who I am is really important and at the heart of the work that I'm doing and I have to be an instrument that knows how to use these tools that I'm being trained to use."[5]

After a delightful respite at the lodge, you put on your boots and trudge through the tundra once more. The knee-deep snow makes for an arduous journey, but as you walk, the snow begins to recede. Things start to become greener. You leave the tundra behind and eventually find yourself at the edge of a forest. You pause and inhale deeply. You notice the warmth of the air and the way it smells faintly of honey. Under this scent there is the musk of soil and the sharp tang of sap or wick—the sign of green life among trees.

While many of the grieving realms involve the presence of other human beings, in this realm the first living other that you notice is a grove of trees. Their branches bloom and loom large above you with leaves that seem to tickle the sunlit sky itself. You brush your palms against the bark and are met by serrated edges that chafe like sandpaper, and you sense a deep knowing from the aged trees. As you trek deeper into the forest you notice the variety of foliage. To your left you see a wood of mighty pines; to your right both palms and cacti tower above. You slowly make your way deeper into the grove, and when you reach the center, you gasp before the Tree of Life.

In the middle of the glade resides the tree of your life—the tree you find most resonant. This mythic tree looks different to each gazer. For Larisa, the Tree of Life looks similar to the giant oak that lives within the moon in the infamous video game *Legend of Zelda: Majora's Mask*. For Justine, this mother of trees looks like none other than the aged White Tree of Gondor from *The Lord of the Rings*. Pale and barren, but nonetheless powerful. Regardless of how you picture the Tree of Life, we invite you to recall that the Tree of Life is an archetype symbolizing the dual nature of life and death, birth and creation—the life force that changes form but never function.

We invite you to pause for a moment with your Tree of Life. Have a seat at its "feet," and consider it carefully. Notice what strikes you, without assigning any judgment to what you find. There are no better or worse trees than any others. Consider taking a moment to meditate under your tree, as the Buddha did beneath the Bodhi tree. Trees are places of deep spiritual meaning and potential. The Tree of Life has close ties with the myth of the philosopher's stone, an allegory depicting the path a human being can take toward enlightenment and wisdom. Trees also have close ties to another human symbol: the age-old family tree depicting generations of both biology and cultural legacy.

This realm of kin carries with it all of the complications of legacy and generations of attachment. As we consider how we both attach and grieve the absence of attachment, we invite you to keep in mind the complicated network of tree roots. When we look at trees in a forest, we typically consider them to be separate, but they're actually connected to one another. With the help of their fungi friends, trees establish linkages, allowing them to share resources and communicate information. Forests are, in so many ways, alive and attached. Similarly, we typically view the ties that connect human beings as largely ephemeral, but under the surface they are vital routes of connection and communication.[6]

Legacy Burdens

Your kin—our term in this realm for your *chosen family* —are those who are connected to you via intimate social ties that you've chosen to build, regardless of whether these folks are connected to you by genetics. It's quite common for folks to think that kinship networks will be less problematic than their family of origin because we chose these people, and surely we chose them because they were kinder or gentler or perceived as "better" in some way than those to whom we were born. But of course, sometimes we choose folks who feel familiar to our internal system because of *homeostasis;* in other words, we gravitate toward what feels familiar, even when it harms us. If we notice that we are in homeostasis, we must get curious about whether those relationships are serving us, or whether parts of us are trying to work out old wounds with new people.

As you sit under your tree, you consider those whom you've chosen to be part of the tree of your life. This might include your partner and their family, as well as friends, community members, beloved animal family members, plants, your surrounding physical environment, or stories.

You and your community collaboratively define your kinship ties.[7] Consider whether anything comes up for you around your family of origin when you reflect on your kin. Just notice, without assigning any judgment to what you find. It's neither good nor bad; it simply exists.

If you find that family-of-origin feelings arise when reflecting on your kin, this is an invitation to pay attention. This could indicate that you chose these kin because of parts of you that hold feelings from your family. These feelings could even indicate an unwanted "gift" from your family line, known as a *legacy burden*. Legacy burdens are burdens that our parts hold that were handed down through the generations. Such burdens are passed down like a family heirloom, regardless of whether the recipient would like to inherit them or not.[8] Just like heirlooms, sometimes the story of where the burden came from gets lost. The item becomes something that exists as an unquestioned part of our lives. We're often left to wonder whether we chose this item or if it was given to us. When considering legacy burdens, you must work with the parts of your inner system to discover what your family gave you and how to pass it back if you don't want it.

Legacy burdens can influence or even dictate how we choose our kin. For example, Larisa is the descendant of Eastern European immigrants, and her paternal great-grandfather was an orphan. One of the legacy burdens she inherited from her great-grandfather was a fear of being seen: to be present and noticed was dangerous for a Polish child who looked like a Jew but was raised in a Catholic orphanage. When she was a small child, her father told her stories praising her great-grandfather's ability to blend in and hide. As an adult, Larisa held onto this legacy burden around hiding and shape-shifting. This led her to choose to have only a small, close-knit group of friends, and a professional career where she knows a great deal about her clients' lives and stories but shares only a limited amount about herself. During the early period of her career, she remained hidden while working in the therapy room, and it was only with the support and guidance of both her own personal therapist and her supervision consultation group that she slowly learned how to show up fully as herself, first in her personal life and then in her professional life.

Healing legacy burdens is not in the purview of this book, but grieving the fact that you have them is very much within the scope of these pages. As therapists, we are likely very familiar with clients expressing sadness, anger, and fear about having to do the work of therapy. Who among us has not heard some version of: "They were the ones who hurt me. It's bad enough to have lived through that, but now I have to *deal* with it." Just as you give your client space to be with these very understandable feelings, we invite you to take some time right now to give yourself space around a similar feeling or set of feelings.

It's not fair. We do the work of sitting with our clients' feelings, and perhaps our supervisees' and students' feelings, on a regular basis. Why do we have to sit with our own? Why is our partner or best friend or new family member asking us to sit with our feelings or their feelings?

Here we are back to the challenging work of our chosen family: if we only give space and energy to our clients' feelings, then we won't have any space or energy for our own feelings, let alone our chosen family's feelings. It's very common for therapists to avoid their own grief by filling up their day with their client's pain. And it's just as common for the first signs of this tendency to arise with the folks with whom we live, be they platonic or romantic. You might at first feel resentful of these kin, as Larisa did when her husband asked her to talk about his fears during the early part of the COVID-19 pandemic. Larisa didn't want to hear about his fears because they reminded her of her own. So, for a time, Larisa just worked, and when she wasn't working she stared at the digital fireplace. In retrospect, Larisa holds deep appreciation for her partner, who continued to advocate for his relational needs, and who invited her to start paying attention to her own.

America's Legacy Burden

Harry Aponte reminds us of the power of asking the community what it needs, rather than leading with judgements or assumptions. Harry centers the person of the therapist, explaining that if "we don't feel our pain as therapists we either cannot feel with our client, or we risk being overwhelmed in session and either freezing or acting out in a destructive way."[9] We offer that this risk applies to both small and large relational groups as well as relational systems.

Let's turn our gaze now to one such large group: American government. The relational system of American government is but one of many systems that affect our lives. What are the other social, cultural, or spiritual systems that flow through you? While it might at first seem strange to spend so much time on systems in the Realm of Our Kin, these systems shape our beliefs, our values, and the very language we speak. They can keep us separated, or they can guide us to our kin; they can support us as we connect, or they can limit our ability to know ourselves and the chosen family to whom we belong.

In the United States, contemporary representative democracy has devolved into rule by wealthy career politicians and judges. The needs of the few are prioritized, and the needs of the many have no legislative voice. This might be hard to sit with, and yet when we turn our eyes to the founding of America, we see those fabled founding fathers holding their own legacy burden. Using Harry Aponte's wisdom to guide us, let's try to better understand the ways the chosen community of the founding fathers came to be. Forged amid the crumbling dynasties of Britain, France, and Spain, this legacy burden encompasses the belief that civilization requires enslavement of an "other"—be it organic or mechanical—to function. These men may very well have been sincere in wanting to create "a more perfect union," but they were constrained by the legacy burden they held—and which they did not pass back, but carried forward—in language that denied the rights of women, queer and trans folks, people of color, and those who didn't own land. We continue to feel the impact of this legacy burden in contemporary America. Our country's federal government is managed and maintained by outliers who decide what the majority of people need with regards to health care, marriage, childcare, eldercare, natural resources, and basic bodily autonomy.

Those in positions of power sometimes divest themselves of parts of their humanity in order to do the work they're asked to carry out. They do this not because they don't care or have never cared, but because becoming part of the system of postindustrial civilization leaves little room for human emotion. If you choose to live in the United States, or if you do not have the resources to leave the United States, then you live in a system that's still governed by this legacy burden. Though you may desperately try to pass it back, the hard answer is that you cannot. It is systemically inescapable. These are not your burdens. However, you may have your own legacy burdens around these historical events, and these you very much can begin to unburden.

While systemic power is a very real force, so too is your authentic voice. The invitation is to acknowledge that you're within a system you can't change alone; and yet, you can make small changes that profoundly impact those with whom you engage. You get to choose kin who share your worldview, or at least your desire to engage in a way that is not consumed by the legacy burdens of others. The more you're able to see yourself as separate but still connected to this system, the more you'll be able to make Self-led choices about your kin.

You take a moment to breathe and lift your gaze to the dappled sunlight shining through the branches (and perhaps leaves, if your tree has them). You listen to the sound of the wind as it moves through the sacred grove, noticing how it whispers through the pines, scratches among the cacti, and waves through the palms. You place your hands on either side of your lap and feel the heat of the earth's soil radiating through the grass and into your skin. You imagine the intricate interweaving of roots and fungi that create a magnificent web far below your hands, and you see yourself connected to your Tree of Life and all other creatures everywhere.

Neighborhood Kinship

In the United States, only one type of chosen family—the nuclear family—is publicly seen and acknowledged as inherently worthy of rights, and thus is provided with structural supports like legal marriage, tax breaks, and family medical leave. But what about the relationship you foster with your elderly neighbor who watches your cats while you're out of town, and whose groceries you carry? What about platonic best friendships that foster lifelong connection and understanding? These and many other nonnuclear relationships are important parts of our kinship network that mainstream society rarely acknowledges and that state and federal government are only just beginning to systemically support.

You may grieve this lack of visibility for the kinship networks you value. There is both sadness and real economic hardship that comes from the lack of systemic support around unmarried and nonbiological chosen-family networks. However, in this sadness, we invite you to pause and ask yourself if you've internalized this lack of recognition of the value of your kinship networks so thoroughly that you, too, struggle to see their importance. For example, when Justine was an undergraduate, she made the dean's list several times, and each time she was invited to a celebratory event that allowed her to bring a "family member." She and her partner were unmarried, so she would often introduce him as her fiancé even though they weren't engaged, because she felt stigma that this person wasn't "really" family, even though the two had lived together for years at that point and were a part of each other's family systems. This is both a small example and a large one because it shows how nefarious the messaging can be: if Justine felt that her romantic heteronormative-presenting partnership wasn't legitimate, then how might a person in a same-gender or polyamorous relationship feel? Such circumstances are even more complex for folks who would like to get married but one or both members of the couple has a disability. Legal marriage can entail losing important financial assistance and health benefits, including Supplemental Security Income and Medicaid, causing some to consider having a ceremony without the legal component. But such a ceremony doesn't provide full resolution either because marriage without the legal documents means having limited access to each other's insurance, losing out on tax breaks, and risking having their partnership viewed as "less than" because it's not a legal marriage.

It's slowly becoming more common for folks to seek opportunities to blend their family of origin with their chosen family. Whether by bringing longtime friends to family events or continuing to include ex-partners in family gatherings, folks are slowly expanding their definition of who belongs. A phrase we, the authors, often use in the therapy space, and that you have already seen a few times in this book, is "verbalize to normalize." Just as powerful is embodying the change or acceptance you want to experience in your community by doing things like introducing your best friend as "your platonic life partner" (Larisa introduces Justine as such on the regular), or designating a close friend as your child's legal guardian if you should die, rather than choosing a biological relative. Some of this messaging might be difficult for your Internal Family Systems to sit with: "But a family is a family!" your system may say, and that makes sense. These are deeply ingrained social constructs, especially about the rules, roles, and boundaries of the family unit. Suddenly these dynamics become even more complicated when you're introducing folks to each other at a barbecue and you say, "This is my sister's ex-wife." Folks may not know how to respond to such a statement, let alone how to interact with your sister's ex-wife.

As you sit under the boughs of your Tree of Life, consider how the interplay between your family of origin and your family of choice shows up in your own life. Look up into your tree's branches and notice which blossoms or leaves spark the most joy for you. Are they parts of your community that you deeply value but tend not to spend the most time with, because you feel compelled (due to societal or personal pressures) to spend time with other branches that just do not spark the same joy? We don't intend to minimize the culturally specific importance of caring for biological elders; however, we do offer that your chosen family gets to be important for you, too. Your chosen kin also gets to be deserving of your time, care, and attention—and they can be lifesaving for you. When biological or immediate family are unavailable or untrustworthy, naming a trusted kinship tie as your emergency contact could literally be the difference between life and death.

Thus we return to the eternal question of what we owe to each other. When you're a helper it can be hard to figure out where the helping ends and the human begins. Our work-life division in America is much different than it was even thirty years ago. Back then the workforce was set up for one partner to work forty hours per week outside the home and for the other partner to work in the home on the tasks of daily living. Our contemporary capitalist hellscape is not set up for two or more people to work outside of the home and navigate chores while also cultivating the emotional and spiritual health of the family.

Because the narratives around sharing lives with more than one working partner are still relatively new, the language to discuss divisions of labor and faith traditions is also lacking. As we have observed in our practices, folks in polyamorous relationships or in communal living situations speak of both the freedom from stereotypical rules, roles, and boundaries, as well as the overwhelm that comes from creating one's own equitable kinship system. This dichotomy can become a source of conflict in homes like these. For helping professionals, many of us are so exhausted at the end of the workday that the idea of having an emotional conversation—or even doing the dishes—feels unmanageable, causing loved ones to believe that we only care for our clients or patients and not for our loved ones.

We live in a society where there aren't enough community resources available for those who need support in caring for their kin, whether those kin are children, aged elders, themselves, or their best friends. This is hard, and it's unfair. You might have grief around the experience of being forced into a caregiving role at home when you're already a caregiver in your work, or you might be grieving what you perceive as unfair labor practices that allow caregivers to take time off that you aren't allowed to take. You may feel resentment that relationships you value and prioritize, such as intimate, platonic friendships, are not legally or socially valued in the same way that marriages or long-term romantic partnerships are valued. Although your initial feeling might be to jump up and run into action, we invite you to continue to sit with these feelings and allow them to be with you and inform you. Rather than attempting to fix or solve, we invite you instead to be fully present with whatever feelings are coming up for you. It is through such patient presence that you will eventually begin to awaken to the work that needs doing.

Let us return to your Tree of Life. As you gaze up into the branches, imagine that each sturdy branch holds a member of your caring community. Though American mainstream society does not always value these connections, sitting together in the Tree of Life is a concrete reminder of both the importance and the strength of these connections. You will likely feel a complex confluence of emotions as you picture these metaphorical connections made literal. You might notice some feelings of sadness or loneliness as you notice empty branches—empty because they represent either beings who have died, friends you have yet to make, or folks with whom you no longer directly communicate. As you notice these feelings, we invite you to simply notice, without trying to fix or make excuses for the empty branches. They simply are. Sometimes, a branch must fall for new growth to sprout.

Grieving Tool—Overexplaining

Sometimes when we don't see eye to eye with our loved one, we'll misinterpret their intent. It's easy to assume negative intent, especially when you're upset. We invite you to remember that most humans who love us seek to express neutral to positive intent most of the time. If we can hang on to that understanding, it can make communication easier.

Also, it may be necessary to get very specific in our wording and "overexplain" ourselves. This is something we discuss with clients regularly when they're having communication struggles, and Justine often discusses it with her graduate students. When they ask her, "Well, what do I do in this situation?" she often simply replies: "Just name it and keep naming it," until the other person understands what you're trying to say. Instead of fancy interventions or mind games à la Carl Whitaker, just name the thing that's happening, or name your intent. For example, you might say to your client or partner, "I feel like this is what you're trying to say. Is that right?" Then they get to answer you. When in doubt, spell it out! Or, to quote one of our favorite pirates from fandom: "Talk it through as a crew."

Client

During the pandemic, clients often struggled with the challenge of too much unoccupied time and too little relational energy. As one client put it, "I only see my kid, and I'm craving more time with my friends; but I barely have enough energy to brush my teeth, let alone do my laundry." In times of heightened stress and depleted energy, we are far more prone to misunderstandings and miscommunications that all too quickly escalate into conflict and confrontation.

Leaning into overexplaining—a tool that works exactly like it sounds—forces us to slow down our communication and lean into repetition. For clients struggling with spending too much time with certain members of their family of choice, this helps them make use of all this extra time. For those seeking to repair and renew relationships with a once-close family member of choice, this tool can help clients avoid misunderstandings caused by having insufficient information. For example, when working as a couples therapist Larisa has often observed members of a couple assume that they know each other's emotions and motivations before they have been explicitly conveyed. Particularly when the couple is attempting to show up in new and different ways, such assumptions can backfire, resulting in a failed attempt at more emotionally vulnerable communication. In these instances, Larisa helps the couple to slow down and take turns both listening and explaining in detail their feelings, thoughts, and motivations.

Therapist
We're all struggling with emotional conversation exhaustion. It's hard to motivate

ourselves to be open to yet another conversation about feelings when our clinical work is taking so much emotional energy. Yet our partners, children, neighbors, and friends want to spend time with us and—perish the thought—engage in emotion-based conversation. Overexplaining can help you tell adult kin the struggle you're having being emotionally present, without the risk of them perceiving you as distant or angry. You're just a tired human who has spent so much time being with feelings. So name this!

For therapists with children, this tool can be harder to navigate, because what we share with children must be developmentally appropriate for them to hear. Discretion and discernment are necessary when using this coping strategy with children. You might say something like: "I am here for you, even though I have this migraine. But we can't play drums today because I have this migraine. You are so great at the drums and I really wish I could listen, but I can't right now. How about I watch you play Roblox instead?"

Due North: Self of the Therapist

We invite you to take stock of the present state of your kinship network. If you notice judgment rising up within you, we invite you to make space for that inner critic even as you attempt to see yourself through a more compassionate lens. Sadness and loss irrevocably change our relationships; this is part and parcel of being alive. Loss can help us notice what's valuable to us. It can help us gain insight into what needs care and healing, and perhaps even what needs more space in our lives. If you've lost touch with friends or colleagues because of the tumult of these challenging times, know that you're not alone in this experience. If you feel sadness as you notice this distance that's opened up between you and others, that might mean that at least part of you would like to reach out to some or all of these friends. Your proverbial tree might need some water and sunlight, and to connect with the roots of others. What useful information you've discovered.

You might also notice that some of the tree's branches have begun to wither and that it's time for them to drop off the tree. This can be difficult, and it's also part of the growth process. If you've struggled with making or maintaining adult friendships, you may know that when you realize you no longer vibe with the friends you had previously, it's a grief process all its own. Perhaps the call to action is to let these branches fall even as you hold gratitude for some or all of the time you spent together, and to cultivate new or different relationships. On the other hand, you might feel like such friendships are worth the energy and effort it takes to shift and evolve together, and that this part of the tree simply needs more care and attention.

Consider for a moment how you view the branches of your tree. As you spend time with this thought, also consider whether you feel that you have been bringing your authentic self into a relationship, or whether parts of you lead the way in your kinships. To be authentic is to be vulnerable, and that can be a frightening prospect, but this is the only way toward a more profound bonding. Many folks are afraid to let their authentic selves lead for fear that others won't accept them. We invite you to get curious with yourself about whether you can bring more of your authentic self into your relationships. If that causes some branches to fall from the tree, that simply means it was their time. Having a few strong branches still makes a lovely tree.

For example, Justine made a major change in her life when she decided to move away from yoga teaching. There were a number of close kinship ties who didn't understand or agree with this decision and began to fall away. This was terribly painful for Justine, and her grief was so deep that she tried to keep teaching long after she wanted to stop. In the end, many branches fell, but a few strong ones survived, and new life began to sprout elsewhere in her tree—vibrant life that could not have emerged while the other branches remained.

Due West: Supervision

Even supervisees who are new to the field often anticipate that their biological family or family of origin will be a topic of their supervisory conversations. However, supervisees often don't consider the place or role that their family of choice has in their therapeutic work. Supervision can be the ideal venue to explore therapeutic self-disclosure as it relates specifically to kinship networks. Supervisees can get curious with their supervisor about their own families of choice and explore how they might model this normalizing language in session with clients. If you're a supervisee and you haven't yet given much time or space to your family of choice, supervision can be a safe space to explore this work.

While many of you are likely familiar with the *genogram* —a therapeutic tool that uses the structure of a family-tree diagram to identify familial relationship patterns—you may not be familiar with ways to use this tool to visualize your family of choice, and how this kinship network shows up for you both inside and outside the therapy experience. Empowered with this community knowledge, you can then work with your supervisor on ways to model inclusive language both with colleagues and with clients.

Supervisors, take a moment to assess your relationships with your family of choice, your legacy burdens, and therapeutic self-disclosure. Do you feel prepared to discuss these topics with your supervisees? Think about what you need in order to hold the space such a discussion will require. Remember that supervision is more than case consultation. We must be able to hold space for the entire person who is the therapist. We invite you to turn to our sage in this realm, Harry Aponte, and let him affirm how you already strive to show up as a supervisor. Harry's "person of the therapist" model teaches trainees to explore all parts of themselves when considering how they show up in the therapy room. Harry extends this emphasis into person-of-the-therapist supervision, where he invites supervisors and supervisees to consider the unique aspects of their personhood that they bring to both supervisory and clinical work.[10]

During Larisa's first supervision experience, her supervisor invited her to explore the many different definitions of time given across cultures. Larisa, indoctrinated in the culture of white professionalism that values punctuality and adhering to set schedules, believed that all good clinical work must happen in a span of fifty-three to fifty-six minutes. Larisa's supervisor, an African American man, shared his own experience of time as existing outside the confines of the clock on the wall. He invited her to conceptualize this concept of time as part of her supervisor's lived experience, rather than an abstract measurement devoid of cultural meaning. He challenged her to notice how the culture of capitalist America was reflected in insurance company time management. Larisa's supervisor modeled for her that his concerns were more focused on offering care to clients and finding a natural place to close a session, rather than adhering strictly to the time on the clock. Now that Larisa is a practicing clinician and supervisor, she brings this questioning of American timekeeping constructs into her work. Even though she must abide by insurance-dictated session length, she seeks out opportunities to highlight the arbitrary and artificial nature of this construct for clients and supervisees.

Due East: Education

Students, how's your cohort doing? Our guess is, it's a mixed bag. Cohorts are little families that were not exactly made by choice. You chose to enter grad school, but you didn't choose this exact group of people with whom to learn. Yet here they are, every day, showing up in the varied ways that different people do. We imagine that there are some folks with whom you resonate, and some who drive you up a wall. That will likely always be true. We invite you to sit with the reality that this cohort is not a part of your tree, unless you decide that one or more of the individuals within it are. You will be able to let these branches fall immediately after school if you so choose. Too many students get attached to the idea of the cohort being a forever tree family, and that doesn't need to be the case. This is a short-term situation that will pass unless you choose to hang on to it.

Teachers, it can be hard to have little families coming and going from your classroom every few months. We invite you to remember that this situation is temporary and to offer as much compassion as possible to your students and their feelings of attachment to cohort outcomes. Cohorts have been struggling with the many collective traumas of this time, and they're acting out in the ways that all families do, each person trying to find their place in the cohort family system. In fact, sometimes smaller family coalitions are formed within the cohort.

Each semester Justine asks her students to do role-plays in small groups to enact different MFT theories. And each semester, some of these small groups bond and become part of one another's trees; for others, the exercise is excruciating as family-of-origin dynamics from each group member play out in real time. One role-play group found that each member was seeing their family of origin reflected back at them through their group members, both during role-plays and during their feedback. This group sought support from Justine, who guided them toward the new information that their "assigned" kin was helping them understand something about themselves and their history. When you navigate similar conversations and dynamics in the classroom (whether virtually or in person), we invite you to remain in as much Self energy as you can. You might practice being firmly rooted like the roots of the tree so the students can scamper all over the branches like squirrels until they find their footing. These saplings don't yet have the skills that you possess as a more mature tree.

Due South: Death and Love

Perhaps one of the more poignant aspects of building a kinship network that doesn't conform to mainstream American definitions of family is navigating the death of chosen kin. Whereas even the most utilitarian HR departments allow one to three paid days off from work when a nuclear family member such as a spouse/legal partner or parent dies, the same cannot be said for the death of a best friend or the death of a beloved animal family member. In such scenarios, not only are you reeling from the loss of a family member, but you are now forced to define and legitimize this loss at a time when what you need is unsolicited compassion and understanding.

During the second year of the COVID-19 pandemic, Larisa's dog, Meronym—beloved by neighbors, Larisa's therapy clients, cat friends, and human family members—became ill with cancer and died within a month of her diagnosis.

Meronym's sudden death was a loss felt by her entire community. As Larisa prepared to take time away from work to care for Meronym in her final days, she communicated clearly to clients that she was taking time away due to a family emergency. However, when it came to her clinical team, she was more transparent about the reasons for her absence. Shortly after notifying her staff via email, a colleague replied via email to thank Larisa for her microactivism at the large private practice where they both worked: "Pets really are like family and I can't imagine how difficult this is. I really appreciate your transparency."

As so often happened during the early years of the pandemic, Meronym's illness coincided with Larisa's entire family of origin being diagnosed and treated for COVID-19. When notifying her colleagues of the need for her absence, Larisa could have kept things generic by referring to a family emergency, or she could have only disclosed the humans who were ill by way of explanation. But the truth was that Larisa was taking time off to be with her dying animal family member. She decided to use her role as the practice's chief of clinical staff to verbalize to normalize. So she explicitly told her staff that she was taking time away to care for Meronym, a member of her chosen family.

6

THE REALM OF OUR REPUBLIC

What is necessary is to once more consider life from the perspective of the Other, of the relationship with the Other, and to afford the Other an ethical precedence—indeed, to relearn the language of responsibility, to listen to the Other and respond.

—BYUNG-CHUL HAN[1]

Our guides for this realm are, at first glance, oddly matched. Swiss psychiatrist Elisabeth Kubler-Ross is the creator of the model of the six stages of grief (denial, bargaining, anger, depression, acceptance,[2] meaning-making[3]) and a passionate advocate of the hospice model. She is joined by contemporary philosopher Byung-Chul Han, a German citizen of South Korean origin. Byung-Chul is a critic of all things connected to neoliberalism,[4] including modern psychotherapy.[5] Perhaps it is fitting that in this region of politics you are supported by these two divisive figures. Though they might not have known one another in real life, in our headcanon we imagine them forging a fraught but lasting bond.

It's time to take our leave of the Tree of Life and the majestic forests of the Realm of Our Kin. As you shoulder your rucksack, you take one final look around this forest of aged pine and swaying maple. You pause to thank this realm for the truths you've gleaned and the meaning you've made. As you peruse your map of the realms of grief, you see greater detail and increased topographic information. You turn your face to the sun and notice the mountains in the distance.

As you walk toward these towering peaks, you realize that you're not alone. Above you in a tree, tucked in so snugly that you can barely see him, is a pygmy owl with feathers the same color as the bark of the tree in which he is nestled. You grin up at his severe expression. A rustling near your feet calls your attention to the ground, and you spot a brown and faintly white spotted rat sniffing at your boots. Your heart jolts, and you look back up at the owl, but he doesn't seem a bit bothered by the rat's presence. In fact, you could swear that the pygmy owl blinks his yellow eyes at the rat as if in hello while the rat stares up and twitches his whiskers at the owl. You might be thinking: "What a delightful odd couple!"

You bend down and offer the rat your hand; it would be an awfully long walk up the mountain on such short legs. The rat hesitates at your outstretched palm, so you rifle through your rucksack until you find a leftover biscuit from your time at the cabin. At the first whiff of biscuit, the rat jumps happily into your hand and nibbles on the biscuit edges. You set the rat on your shoulder, and he promptly snuggles into your muffler, his whiskers softly tickling your ear. The owl is intrigued now as well and flaps to a closer branch to have a look. Again, you're worried that he might eat the rat, but once more they simply observe one another with curiosity. The owl flaps to another branch, and you realize that he's following you as you move. It seems you have companions for your trip to the base of the mountain.

You and your companions take the unmarked trail to your right—you and the rat on foot, the pygmy owl on wing, pausing on branches as he sees fit. You consider what a strange and beautiful thing it is that these natural enemies have found peace in your company and on this journey. As you begin to climb, you reflect on the divisions between people in your own life. You consider how politics have divided the country and, in turn, people you love and people in your therapy office. We have all experienced sitting across (whether physically or virtually) from a client who is sharing something about their political views that we find upsetting, or even abhorrent. It can be difficult to continue to hold the therapeutic space as a client reflects that they believe that one's sex or gender or sexual or romantic orientation make them less deserving of rights.

You continue to climb and notice the gentle chittering of Rat near your ear. Owl swoops low overhead as if to check in on his friend. You marvel at this blossoming interspecies dynamic and then consider that perhaps they've been friends for years. Just because you're new to their dynamic, that doesn't mean their relationship is new to them. You reflect on thoughts of perspective, difference, self, and other as you move higher up the mountain.

Political Division

The years following the 2016 US presidential election brought with them visible divisions that had never before been seen in living memory. While there are always divides between generations and across political aisles, aggressive rhetoric and a lack of compassionate discourse became the norm, growing into virulent arguments, cutoffs, and internet trolling. Consider for a moment what your experience was like with friends, family, and colleagues during this time, and what it's been like since then. Perhaps you have lost or intentionally disconnected from folks with whom you were once close. Depending on your own intersection of identities, you may have found that you couldn't have compassion for groups of people who were actively engaged in taking away your rights, or who agreed with those who did. Friends and family who remained on the sidelines may have hurt you still more with their silence. Perhaps you actively took steps within your own clinical practice to either clarify your political opinions with current and prospective clients, or you decided to both clarify and then refer out those clients with whom you felt strong political divergence.

No matter what your decision was at the time, we suspect that it was a difficult one to make. Or rather, if it felt righteous in the moment, then perhaps what followed were feelings of guilt, shame, and sadness around the choices you made when feeling activated. We bring this up not as a provocation but rather as an invitation for you to get curious about the grief inherent in the choices you felt called to make. Regardless of where you are on this journey, we invite you to make space for the undoubtedly conflicted thoughts and feelings you have around the idea of cutoff, referring clients out due to disparate political beliefs, appropriate therapeutic disclosure, and continuing to work with clients whose beliefs and life experiences are radically different from your own.

As you breathe into this emotional space, you might notice thoughts or feelings stepping forward that hold memories of either distance or cutoff from important friends and family. Recall our conversations in chapters 4 and 5 surrounding Internal Family Systems. Even when you're physically distant or cut off from a close friend or family member, part of them remains within your system. Those of you familiar with Murray Bowen's family systems work surrounding triangles, cutoff, and differentiation will no doubt recall his staunch belief in never cutting off a close friend or family member. While in today's world this might seem extreme, Bowen advocated for distance rather than cutoff because he believed staying in relationship helped the individual learn about their family and themselves, allowing for eventual differentiation from the family or system of origin.

Of course, those closest to us can cause the most pain. In addition, the greater collective can be an important part of our daily lives. With the rapid change in societal discourse and the rights of women, people of color, queer and trans folks, and victims of abuse being taken away, it can feel as though society is trying to cut you off, and you may want to cut them off in turn. This state of affairs invites folks to limit those with whom they engage, and each of our worlds get smaller and more compartmentalized. We offer no judgment here, but we do invite you to consider what is lost when we shut ourselves off from one another and the world around us.

Perhaps as you sit with this thought, you notice a part or parts of you having a strong feeling. You might notice an internal pull to reject this idea, communicated in some form of the following statement: "Why should I care when [insert person or group name] doesn't care at all about me?" While therapist parts may then chime in with reminders about compassion fatigue and empathy exhaustion, we invite you to be present with any and all parts that are rejecting this idea of being present with the other. It is incredibly painful to feel disowned or rejected by a group. One of the main results of our increased political division is that the threat of being excommunicated from the group and being deprived of access to vital care is ever increasing. This situation taps into our primal fear of being cast out of the tribe to survive in the wilderness all alone, which of course is impossible. Thus, to be cast out is to be sent to our doom. We invite you to sit with a hard question: Is your fear of being cast out motivating you to cast out others? Or to run from a relationship before you can become close enough to be threatened by the risk of disownment?

As always, this is simply an invitation to notice, not a stick with which to beat yourself. Whatever you find is simply information to help you decide what you'd like to do or change moving forward.

Self and Other

Midway up the mountain path, you and your guides decide to take a lunch break beside a stream. The sound of the water bubbling over small rocks and smooth pebbles relaxes you, and you mindfully ease your shoulders down your back as you sit beside the creek. Rat hops down off your shoulder and begins sniffing at your rucksack as if to request more biscuits please. Owl flaps his tawny brown wings flecked with white, and lands on a nearby log. You search in your rucksack and find two more biscuits and a bright summer orange. You divide the two biscuits evenly between the three of you, and offer a slice of orange each to Rat and Owl. Owl peers at the piece of orange, poking at it with one long golden talon. Rat seems happier about the prospect of this citrus snack and begins to eat a small hole right through the center of his slice.

Again you reflect on how something so simple can bring the most disparate of companions together for a compassionate lunch, and you wonder what it might be like if only the outside world could learn some of the lessons of the mountain. As you enjoy these quiet moments with your new friends, you realize the radical nature of this experience: a rat, a pygmy owl, and a human sitting beside a babbling brook, sharing a lunch together.

How might we bring a radical community into the therapy space? As our political systems fracture, you may want to consider ways to bring your honest self into all aspects of your life, up to and including the therapy room. This can feel both complicated and confusing because therapy school teaches us to check our activism—and our love of anime—at the therapy room door.

This social construct is far overdue to be challenged. The Freudian idea that therapists are supposed to be tabula rasas for their clients is long past its usefulness in the context of the modern and postmodern theories from which most therapists work.

Though Byung-Chul Han is no fan of modern therapy,[6] throughout his work he conveys profound respect for and belief in the healing power of genuine listening. His conception of a true dialogue between Self and Other vividly recalls the therapeutic dynamic between therapist and client when the therapist is wholly present:

> Listening is not a passive act. It is distinguished by a special activity: first I must welcome the Other, which means affirming the Other in their otherness. Then I give them an ear. Listening is a bestowal, a giving, a gift. It helps the Other to speak in the first place. It does not passively follow the speech of the Other. In a sense, listening precedes speaking; it is only listening that causes the Other to speak. I am already listening before the Other speaks, or I listen so that the Other will speak. Listening invites the Other to speak; it frees them for their otherness. The listener is a resonance chamber in which the Other speaks themselves free.[7]

It is only by knowing and embodying ourselves fully as human therapists that we can heal through listening.

The task before us is one of integration. We must integrate radical political presence into our therapeutic approach. The first step in this process is to spend time exploring your political beliefs and values, as well as the experiences that led you to hold these beliefs and values. This may be an opportunity for parallel processing with clients who also wish to bring their political journey into the therapeutic space. Part of what separates this process from political activism is that, as a clinician, you're not attempting to convince, convert, or cajole your client into agreeing with your political perspective. As you invite your client to explore the meaning of politics in their life, you'll be tasked with exploring your own political beliefs, motivations, and values outside the therapy room. Through journaling, self-reflection, consultation, or conversation with trusted friends you can get curious about the many experiences that have led to your own political perspective. In so doing, you'll have the energy and emotional space necessary to support your client on their political journey.

Consider our guides on the mountain path. Rat is not attempting to grow wings and join Owl in flight, but Owl and Rat are enjoying a biscuit together, each as their own discrete selves. Owl is able to be present with Rat, perhaps because he is sitting with his own internal drives or instincts to see Rat as prey, that is, food. It is honest presence with his parts, rather than repression of his instincts, that allows Owl to forge a friendship (or at least a compassionate presence) with Rat. The second step in this process is to decide how you'll embody your beliefs in the therapy space. Remember that this need not be an act of conversion on your part, but rather inviting a part of you into the space to authentically reflect who you are. When therapists discuss informed consent with their clients, the discussion is often incomplete because the client doesn't fully know the person with whom they're consenting to share all their darkest secrets. Something Justine does in her practice—which she admittedly has the freedom to do as a solo practitioner—is to be very open with her authentic self in all of her marketing and advertising, including her website. That way a prospective client will have a good sense of who Justine is as a human before they decide to contact her.

    The final step in this process is grieving. This grief will be specific to the clinician and will depend on your own areas of systematic marginalization and your personal experiences of individual and systemic oppression and abuse. You may find that you need a supportive community with whom to grieve, comprising both colleagues and friends. Yet again we find ourselves in a realm where so much is asked of us as therapists while so little systemic support is offered to us. As with all the realms we are visiting, there is no map for how to create this kind of community. We invite you to reach out to the colleagues from whom you've sought support in the past and see about creating a group within which you can all share the griefs with which you have struggled. Consider creating a group based on the type of therapy you practice or the particular griefs with which you have struggled.

Federal politicians and Supreme Court justices, both in positions of great political power, likely do not consider the impact their legislation and rulings have on the mental health of the folks they govern, or the additional strain their decisions impose on mental health and medical professionals. Perhaps you notice a wave of anger washing over you right now, followed quickly by a tsunami of sadness and exhaustion. Elisabeth Kubler-Ross reminds us that death and loss can feel profoundly unfair.[8] Anger, Elisabeth believed, was a valuable and necessary emotion, especially in times of loss, because it can propel you deeper into feeling the many varied emotions that come from loss: "Anger affirms that you *can* feel, that you *did* love, and that you have lost."[9] To her, anger was not a time of meaning-making but of deep and present feeling. Through such confrontation with your own feelings, a path toward meaning can begin to take shape.[10]

For moments such as these, we, the authors, offer you compassion and an example of the ways we make meaning from such moments. We cannot presently do the work of political leaders and judges, but we can do our work as clinicians to the very best of our abilities, which means being ready to meet the political moments that show up in our therapy rooms. These moments of person-to-person connection are meaningful. Often we focus on the large moments of activism such as marches and sit-ins, but much of the change that occurs in the world is through small acts of engagement, person to person. You believe this, too; we know you do, because you're a therapist.

Up ahead, you see the summit. As you and your two mercurial companions ascend this mountain of political grieving, you notice that your limbs start to become heavy. With each step, it's harder to take a breath. You feel the pressure of the altitude. At first, you fight against these somatic (i.e., physical) feelings. You are so close to completing this realm. You think of the map and the feeling of calm and relief that comes from a completed job. But these are not your present feelings. In this moment, you realize that you're feeling the weight of sadness. It sits like boulders in your rucksack.

The work of political reckoning in the therapy room is both valuable and important. It is also more work. It's not fair that we're asked to do so much. We carry more than our fair share, and folks don't realize that. But reader, we want you to know that we see you. We see you carrying the burdens of the world on your shoulders, and it's okay when it feels too heavy.

Whatever your political beliefs, we invite you to sit with the sadness of our present political moment, when we need so much both collectively and individually, and we feel like we have no more to give. So much is already asked of the therapist, the supervisor, the teacher, the student; yet the reality of life is that we all need to be doing regular political engagement for the community to function. But in our current times, political engagement is ever more demanding and emotionally taxing.

Grieving Tool—Tea with Your Shadow

As narrative therapists we incorporate both IFS and Jungian techniques into our therapy practice. The grieving tool "tea with your shadow" marries the Jungian concept of the shadow self with the IFS technique of sitting down with a challenging part of your consciousness in an attempt to get to know it better. This tool invites clinicians to sit down with the political aspect of their shadow self. Few things are more clinically challenging than working with a client who does not share your political perspective. Sitting down with your own biases can give you valuable information about the experiences and emotions that drive these beliefs, allowing you to be more informed about and supportive to your clients. Having tea with your shadow can be a humbling process that fosters systemic parallel processing inside and outside the therapy space. In other words, the intrapersonal change within the clinician shifts interpersonal dynamics in the therapy room.

Client

The Jungian shadow—the hidden, unconscious part of the self that contains the aspects of a person from which their consciousness hides—is often triggered by politics. Jung described the shadow like this: "It is a frightening thought that man also has a shadow-side to him, consisting not just of little weaknesses and foibles, but of a positively demonic dynamism. The individual seldom knows anything of this; to him, as an individual, it is incredible that he should ever in any circumstances go beyond himself."[11]

In modern America, both Democrats and Republicans often collude with their respective party politicians and political structures to avoid facing uncomfortable realities. How a client responds to a current political issue, such as COVID-19 mask mandates, not only gives you important information about their political perspective; it also hints at the parts of themselves they may be avoiding. These hidden parts, often synonymous with exiles in a traditional IFS perspective, make up the shadow side of a person's identity. A client who refuses to wear a face mask and who is angry about mask mandates may have a shadow self who seeks individual control because it fears the powerful pull of the collective community. One of the founding myths of America is the autonomous pioneer or yeoman who made a name, a home, and a land for themselves without help of others. But part of what makes this American myth endure is the shadow of European serfdom, which prized community over individual well-being except for a rarefied rich elite.

"Tea with your shadow" invites clients to notice the person or group of people with whom they have a political disagreement and then encourages the client to consider this person or group from a place of curiosity. To borrow again from Jung, the client's anger over the mask mandate is actually the client's anger and fear of their own shadow—in this case, a collection of parts that seeks the comfort of servitude and devotion to another. In therapy, it's often necessary to create imaginary dialogue between the client and their shadow—in this case, the perceived enforcer of the mask mandate—before they can see and sit down with their shadow self.

Therapist

As therapists, you are likely familiar with both the idea and the practice of engaging with the memories, feelings, and parts evoked for you in your clinical work. The grieving tool "tea with your shadow" takes this common practice one step further in that it encourages you to practice conceptualizing your shadow self as a discrete part of yourself with whom you can have a dialogue. We are often in secret conflict with our shadow because it holds ideas, values, and experiences that our conscious parts have been taught to eschew. It's not uncommon for a therapist's shadow to be quick to judgment, anger, and retribution because as clinicians we're taught to value and to practice curiosity, calm, and compassion.

For Larisa, making a regular practice of sitting down with her acerbic shadow has proved helpful throughout her career. During the early phase of her clinical training, she struggled with "bringing home" the feelings stirred up in her therapy sessions, sometimes resulting in case conceptualizing and research long into the night. It also resulted in her withdrawing from friends and family because she couldn't talk to them about what was consuming her—her clients—for fear of breaching confidentiality. Larisa learned to use consultation and supervision to process clinical sessions, and her shadow became a crucial part of her learning how to shift out of her therapy role and into the many roles of her personal life. She made a practice of spending her commute home engaging with art that would bring out her more critical and cynical shadow, which helped her disengage from her therapy parts and give herself permission to be something other than a compassionate mountain.

Following Larisa's move to Chicago and her shift to fulltime private practice, her shadow proved helpful once again in navigating sessions with clients who hailed from the realm of conservative politics. Although it may sound surprising, Larisa's shadow contains a great many conservative values, not the least of which is that marriage is for life, with no exceptions. Larisa's Self and many of her other parts disagree with this value, but her shadow holds to it. In working with this internal discord and learning to make space for it rather than forcing a dialectical synthesis that would only sublimate her shadow rather than integrating it, Larisa grew in her compassion and understanding for her clients who held conservative values. Currently, she seeks to work collaboratively with the parts of her that hold conservative values as well as those parts that hold socialist values. While this pairing may strike some as unique bordering on oxymoronic, Larisa finds this challenge to be helpful for her personal and professional growth. Her internal community holds a dialectical truth that she uses to support her clients and her Internal Family System.

Due North: Self of the Therapist

Bringing your authentic self into the therapy room is a radical act, and it is not without challenges. The biggest challenge happens when you and your client have disparate political views, causing tension in the room. We invite you to pause for a moment and consider your experiences with political division in therapy. Was it your instinct to immediately refer your client out to another provider, or did you work it into the therapy space?

Justine considers herself liberal in her political beliefs. She engages a third-wave feminist lens and is committed to creating spaces of antiracism and antioppression in therapy and academia. Over the years, she has had clients whose views were diametrically opposed to some or all of these values. In those instances, Justine got curious about why the client was coming to see her. As mentioned above, Justine is vocal about who she is and what she believes, in the hopes of offering clients true informed consent about working with her. One client in particular asked Justine if she felt she could be objective in working with him, because he was a men's rights activist. This term refers to someone who believes that men are marginalized in Western culture and who blames their challenging circumstances on the power they perceive women have over them in contemporary society. This client came to Justine seeking support around a mental health issue and wanted to be sure she would not discriminate against him because of his beliefs.

Although Justine was taken aback, she shared that she does have expertise in the areas in which the client was seeking support, explaining that as long as he was open to the idea that they differed greatly in some of their beliefs, she could absolutely help him with his mental illness. Did she sometimes bristle at a comment from the client about how he saw the world? Yes, she did. And because they had discussed it, she could name it and bring that experience into the room, using language like: "Wow, client, I just had a reaction to that comment you made about that group of people. Could you say a bit more about how that relates to your mental health?" This interplay became a powerful part of their therapeutic relationship, and Justine got the opportunity to see this person's vulnerability.

Justine found that she needed to do her own processing around what this client brought up for her Internal Family System, and she spent time in consultation with trusted colleagues who helped her continue to return to her Self energy and meet the client as a human being rather than an opponent. We want to point out that working with clients who hold diametrically opposed views was not always easy for Justine. While she was growing up, her father was the mayor of their town for sixteen years, and she had unwittingly formed an attachment to and reverence for

Democratic political leaders. Due to this allegiance, she struggled to even see differences of opinion within the liberal sphere. It took her spending much time with her internal family to sort this out and understand that differences of opinion were not threats to her identity.

We invite you to pause and sit with the thoughts and feelings coming up for you in response to this story. Notice what bubbles up in your body when we offer that politics has a place in the therapy space. Without any judgment, just notice what is present or what steps forward. What do you observe? Was any of it from the stages of grief? Perhaps you notice that you are in denial of this being possible for you to do; perhaps you are feeling sad and experiencing ambiguous loss for the therapist you were taught to be in school (the blank slate); or perhaps you are feeling angry at us for asking you to do so much internal work. Whatever is there, simply let it be. Consider whether there is anything you would like to leave here on the mountain, or if there is anything new you would like to pick up and take with you as you continue onward. We, the authors, consider it clinically significant to bring the political into the therapy room because it is naturally already there. If we define politics as the conversation, construction, and operation of governing systems that are both acted upon and enacted by human beings, then the answer becomes clear. Both your own and your clients' bodies are political, and you bring them into the therapy space each time session begins.

While we, the authors, value the personal and therapeutic growth that can come from this type of challenging clinical dynamic, we also recognize that doing this work effectively often takes enormous time and energy. If you decide to continue working with a client whose political views are anywhere from moderately to highly disparate from your own, you'll need to seek regular consultation, either weekly or every other week. You'll likely also spend time processing your personal feelings and reactions related to such a case in your own personal therapy. You may have to make changes to your direct client care schedule to account for prep time and decompression time before and after sessions with these types of clients. This investment of time, energy, and resources may not be possible for you, or it may mean keeping a smaller number of these types of clients on your caseload.

You might remember from therapy school that whatever we do not mention in the therapy room is something that our clients consider to be either unwelcome or unimportant in this relationship. If we do not, for example, acknowledge our client's class and financial status, immigrant status, chronic illness, or disability (which—spoiler alert—is political), then we're not looking at our clients or ourselves as being fully human, living within the confines of a system.

We are instead conceiving of them as living in a vacuum. Acknowledging that politics is involved in therapy does not always mean engaging in political action or activism in the therapy room. It does mean always being honest with yourself about who you are, what you believe, and what you're capable of. This type of therapeutic social modeling invites your client to do the same. To use language that our sage Byung-Chul Han can understand, the therapy room is the space where the self and the other engage in meaningful and often transformational dialogue, not because they're trying to convince each other or turn one another into themselves, but because the act of honest and compassionate communion changes each of us.

Due South: Supervision

Supervisees, you are in a unique position to change how you work before you get dug in like some of your more seasoned colleagues. Experience is not everything. Sometimes working for longer in the field means we've had more time to make mistakes and avoid looking at ourselves. At this stage in your early career you get the opportunity to get curious with yourself about who you are authentically and what you want to put out into the world and into the therapy room. It's okay for you to want to bring social justice into the therapy room. It's okay for you to want to bring your whole self into the therapy room. For example, Larisa once had a supervisee who was struggling with how to bring their authentic self into therapy. They asked, "How do I be honest about who I am while keeping the focus on the client?"

Larisa gave what she thought would be a pretty chill answer: "Well, you're already doing that. Your clients know that you like robots." Visibly alarmed, the supervisee asked how Larisa knew this. Larisa explained that since the supervisee had decorated their therapy office with robot statues, both she and their clients had learned that robots were meaningful to this supervisee. Larisa explained that the supervisee could take this one step further and use a robot metaphor to explain a particular therapy skill or coping strategy to a client. "In this way," Larisa said, "you're bringing your authentic love of robots into session while keeping the focus on the client and their therapy work."

Supervisors, how are you supporting your supervisees in their journey of self-exploration? Are you encouraging them to lean into their feelings of outrage and learn from that? Are you getting to know your supervisee as an authentic person, and do you allow that authentic person to be the one in your supervision room. Supervisors, not only are you tasked with engaging authentically with clients on political issues; your supervisees need your help to learn how to do so as well. The supervision relationship is a wonderful space for social modeling. As the supervisor, you will teach your supervisee how to engage in authentic political discussion by initiating these kinds of dialogues during supervision.

It will be important for you to name in supervision when events of a political nature have occurred and check for consent to discuss them. For example, following the murder of Mr. George Floyd by police in May 2020, Larisa began each of her supervision hours by saying a version of the following: "We can spend as much or as little time on this as you need today, supervisee. I acknowledge the recent murder of Mr. George Floyd by the Minneapolis Police Department. Would it be helpful if we held space for this in supervision today? Though we may hold differing perspectives, I hope that you trust that I'm here to hear your thoughts and feelings."

Of course, having said all that, Larisa needed to actually be prepared to hear these authentic thoughts and feelings. Holding space during such supervision hours took enormous emotional energy. After these supervision hours, Larisa had to return to five to seven hours of direct client care. Part of the grief for Larisa during the summer after Mr. George Floyd's death was sitting with how much was being asked of her in this political moment, and how little she had at the end of each day for family and herself.

Due East: Education

Justine had the unique experience of becoming an educator during the pandemic. Although she should have expected that a cohort forced out of the literal world and into the virtual one would show the impact of that trauma, she was nevertheless surprised to discover evidence of it; clearly she'd been hiding it from herself. Justine found that this cohort was profoundly divided over their political views, and without being in a shared space, they were unable to sit with one another and perceive each other as humans. Unfortunately they didn't have the skills needed to navigate this situation, and they were never fully able to heal the wounds they unintentionally caused one another. Depending on where you are in school, you might have experienced a similar situation. It's likely that political discussion is not welcomed in your school experience, as most schools still hold fast to the concept of the tabula rasa. We invite you to consider doing it differently. Your teachers don't know everything.

Teachers, consider how you're allowing the political to enter the education space. We recognize that asking you to do so is putting even more into your rucksack when it's full already. You're underpaid, overworked, and undertrained. You're already doing the work of an educator, a clinician, and a mentor; and yet, the political is already in your classroom. While in some ways we're asking you to do more, in other ways we're asking you to do less. By this we mean that when you show up as your authentic self in the education space and naturally allow political discourse to flow, you don't have to worry about presenting as a blank slate for your students. You have the opportunity to model what it is to be a human who happens to be a therapist. You can show your students that working as a therapist need not become one's sole identity, nullifying any opportunity to share political opinions.

Due South: Death and Love

It's time to complete this hike through the Realm of Our Republic. You straighten your shoulders and lean into the wind as you and your sage companions climb to the summit of this mountain. As you climb, you notice that your face is starting to get wet. Looking up, you see nary a cloud in the cerulean sky. Rat snuggles closer to you, and Owl glides just a few feet from the top of your head. You are not alone in your grieving.

We invite you to give yourself permission to express whatever you're feeling at this moment, whether it's sorrowful tears or cries of anger. If you find the framing device of Elisabeth Kubler-Ross's six stages of grief helpful, you might turn to it now. Although

Kubler-Ross's model doesn't depict the full nuance of individualized grief, it does offer an organizational structure that can be helpful when you're feeling profound overwhelm. We invite you to be present for the ambiguous loss facing the present reality of our industry. However you envisioned political involvement in your clinical work, the reality is likely very different from whatever you imagined. We invite you to grieve the loss of the clinician you thought you would be, as well as the loss of the field of which you thought you were going to be a part.

As you survey the summit, you take out your map and drafting tool, and you fill in the details of this region. What you've learned will help the next generation of explorers be better prepared and better equipped. You might even take a moment to appreciate or recall the parts of this work that you love. Early in her training, one of Larisa's supervisors advised her to keep a record of the moments when she loved her work, explaining: "You'll have bad days and hard days when you won't remember that you're a good or even average therapist. You won't be able to access what you love about this work. Or the joy that it sometimes brings you. Keep a record (HIPAA-compliant, of course) of those moments of meaning."

One of these moments to which Larisa regularly returns is a closing she once had with a client who held a very different political perspective from her own. In this session, the client expressed gratitude for their work together, saying: "You never tried to make me into anything. Your goal was always to help me figure out who I was and how to make choices that resonated with my values."

7

THE REALM OF OUR FAITH

> *It is said that God has created man in his own image. But it may be that humankind has created God in the image of humankind.*
> —THICH NHAT HANH[1]

Religion holds a precarious place in contemporary society. As we prepare to explore the place of faith and spirituality, we want to acknowledge the varied ways in which people engage with these concepts. Some prefer to have—or have had experiences that led them toward—a lack of faith. Just naming "spirituality," though separate from religion, can be triggering. Some swing the pendulum to the opposite end and find a faith tradition to be the cornerstone of their lives, to the exclusion of other aspects. In order to find a place of balance betwixt these many disparate religious perspectives, we once again find ourselves with an unconventional pairing: Vietnamese Buddhist monk Thich Nhat Hanh, father of the mindfulness movement, and artist Pamela Colman Smith, illustrator of the beloved Rider-Waite-Smith tarot deck.

Thich Nhat Hanh was lovingly called Thay (the Vietnamese word for "teacher") by his followers. Beloved not just by Buddhists, Thich Nhat Hanh authored over a hundred books on various aspects of the Buddhist tradition, such as mindfulness and nonattachment, and he made them understandable and applicable so folks from any faith tradition could incorporate them into their lives. Whereas Thich Nhat Hanh embodies the ability to look within oneself and then carry what one finds there out into the world, Pamela Colman Smith embodies the reverse. The art of her tarot deck allows humans to create unique portals into internal contemplation and confrontation with their individual unconscious. A performer and artist in the nineteenth century, Pamela was inspired in equal parts by her paternal legacy of medieval lore and her maternal legacy of Jamaican folktales.[2]

While on the surface, these two sages seem quite different, they share the perspective of spirituality and reflection as active, living, vital processes. Thich Nhat Hanh's mindfulness calls even the most casual of practitioners to action: "Our own life has to be our message."[3] Pamela Colman Smith's artwork is what makes the Rider-Waite-Smith tarot deck so compelling all these decades later. Both of these humans remind us that the original spark of all religions and spiritual practices lies in active meaning-making.

It was a long hike to the summit of Mount Politics. As you survey the map you drew and compare it to the summit upon which you now stand, you notice the shift of a shadow. Looking up at the sky, you see that cloud cover has made way for the bright sun. You shield your eyes and prepare to scout the descent down the other side of the mountain. A dark form extends across your sight line. As you take a few steps forward, you realize that the shadow was not just a trick of the light; rather, the lip of a large hole. You step to the edge of the mountain's gaping maw and peer down into hundreds of feet of cavernous walls and then ... blackness. Whatever lies below is so far down as to defy both the reach of the sun and human eyesight. Perhaps the way forward is not across but through?

Luckily, you planned for just such an event. Digging through your rucksack, you find the climbing rope, carabiners, and headlamp you packed. Working quickly but carefully, you set up a simple pulley system and prepare to lower yourself down into what you are beginning to suspect (or hope?) is an *inactive* volcano. You attempt to reassure Owl and Rat, your intrepid mountain guides, that you'll venture down first, and then they can join you once you know it's safe. Rat sniffs along the edge of hole, making worried chirping noises as he goes. Owl simply stares at you from his perch on a nearby rock. You cannot be certain, but Owl's golden eyes seem more stern than usual. You double-check the batteries on your headlamp as the sun begins to set in the west, turning the distant treetops first gold, then amber, and finally scarlet.

Owl flies from his perch to land next to Rat, who leans into Owl's feathered chest as they settle themselves on the lip of the hole. They'll be all right up here, you think. With a reassuring nod to Owl and Rat, you slowly ease your way over the lip of the crater. You look up at your two guides as you slowly lower yourself down into the darkness. Their faces etched in grave concern, they advise you to be wary of your surroundings. "Don't worry about us, just focus on what's in front of you," advises Rat. While Owl replies, "Death is but a part of life. When we lose death, we cease to be alive and become zombies."[4]

You shake your head ruefully at your guides' ideas of helpful advice and instead direct your focus to the inner walls of the volcano. You gasp as you see drawings on these walls—an intricate series of painted scenes and engravings, curving around the entire chamber that leads to the base of this inactive volcano. As you slowly descend, you realize that these pictures tell the story of human religion, starting from humanity's modern era. You're surprised to see such a depth and breadth of various belief systems, some of which you never would have imagined.

Snaking across the wall you see Q, face obscured, and a finely etched drawing of a laptop computer emanating a series of gold rays, which you assume to symbolize the thousands of posts and blogs that form the basis of the QAnon belief system. The next panel depicts children huddled before a sundial as a lizard-person lunges at a circle of human adults. Some of the faces in the circle seem familiar, while others are totally foreign to you. Below the pictorial story of QAnon, you find panels depicting Scientology, complete with Xenu and his spacecraft, followed by Joseph Smith receiving the book of Mormon via his magic glasses. As the light from above turns into a disk the size of the moon, you see panels depicting Confucian thought and Hindu Goddesses. You notice several depictions of the Tree of Life, and you spot what appears to be several different iterations of the Buddha. You attempt to track the development of Goddess worship down the wall, and you notice that the Goddess religions flourish to the left, while on the right the warrior cults take focus.

It is only when the crater's mouth at the top of the chamber becomes a mere pinprick of light that you spot panels depicting the religions of the sands—Christ, Muhammad, and Moses—farther up the wall. Did you miss them earlier? Or was your sight just overwhelmed by the strangeness of finding a mural of world religions buried deep within the mountainous realm of politics?

Before you can fully contemplate these questions, your feet touch solid ground—magma that has long since cooled. You shout up to your guides and wonder if they can hear you.

Shouldn't they be at least halfway down by now? Perhaps they've decided not to join you here. You feel a sudden sadness and loneliness at this thought. You release your tethers and look around the chamber, expecting to see more panels depicting Gods and Goddesses—evidence of humanity's primal need for meaning-making. But instead all you see are empty walls of varying shades of gray. You gingerly reach out to touch the rock before you and find only stone and ash. The light on your headlamp flickers, and you crane your neck up to try to see ... someone, anyone? You move to shout again, but then you realize: in the realm of faith, you are all alone.

Let There Be Light

It can be scary to be in the Realm of Our Faith, whether you hold your own faith closely in your rucksack, or you believe that religion doesn't belong on the trail. The question of whether or to what extent faith should enter the therapy space is one of the oldest questions in our industry. But one thing is certain: no matter how big or small our faith may be, we're not religious instructors. Even faith-based clinicians are not charged with the task of converting their clients or teaching religion to them. We can support our clients as they explore what their faith means to them, but as time passes and religious expression becomes a more contested part of cultural life, we may find ourselves feeling lost. Once religion was both a governing principle and a source of communal meaning-making. Now it's often a divisive stick with which we beat each other.

We, the authors, imagine Thich Nhat Hanh smiling wryly at us. A person could in fact make the case that contemporary clinicians are indeed religious instructors. Mindfulness skills and nonattachment practices have become all but ubiquitous in the therapy room. Many electronic medical records even list mindfulness skills on a checklist of approved interventions. Perhaps you've already spotted the irony? Mindfulness and nonattachment to outcomes are core Buddhist practices, and they've flourished in American mental health settings (and in many other areas) largely due to the work of Buddhists like Thich Nhat Hanh, who has said, "Mindfulness is the miracle by which we master and restore ourselves."[5] Thanks to Thich Nhat Hanh and other engaged Buddhists' work to bring these concepts into the mainstream and demonstrate their benefit, Buddhism is now a major part of the field of psychotherapy. In a way, many therapists are practicing Buddhists. Let that sink in.

Clinicians and clients need the gravity once brought by religion. Increasingly folks are looking for therapy to fill the role of purpose and meaning that religion once offered them. In America, folks are not engaging with faith in the way they once did, largely because of science, technological globalization, and oppression. Since the time of Galileo, religion and science have been at odds, largely because religious traditions tend to struggle with the idea of multiple versions and interpretations of how humans got here and what we're supposed to be doing now that we are here. Where religious sects were once isolated and cut off from the outside world, now almost everyone has at least partial access to the internet, thanks to public libraries (with the exception of cults who deny this to members). Now folks can more easily find information that doesn't fit with their belief system and prompts them to begin to question the nature of their religious reality. Finally, many of the large religious groups in America have become radicalized and, perhaps in an attempt to maintain their doctrines and systems of belief, have gone the way of fundamentalism, making it all but impossible for queer and trans folks, feminists, punks, polyamorous folks, and any person or family whose behavior doesn't align with that belief system to remain a part of the faith.

For all the potential risks of religious thought and practice, it does excel at uniting folks around a common cause. Religion has always centered itself around questions of meaning and purpose. How do we answer the existential questions of life without faith? Are therapists the best people to help folks answer these questions? Perhaps such questions are beside the point. The reality is that we increasingly find ourselves being asked to help clients find meaning and make purposeful sense of their place in the world. Yet we're already so tired. We find that we miss having community and meaning-making leaders to guide us on this leg of the journey.

In the Realm of Our Faith, this may very well be our first grief: we experience the void once filled by faith healers, religious leaders, and ritual practices. Clients look to us to help them answer some of the deepest questions of life, and that is not exactly what we were trained to do; and yet in some ways it is. If you're a therapist who is committed to the power of meaning-making, ritual, and compassionate presence, then you might consider yourself equipped to work with some of these more existential questions. Consider for a moment how you came to a place where you felt comfortable working clinically with aspects of faith. Ask yourself whether this happened because of something you learned—perhaps somewhere in school, from a mentor, or in your family of origin. Think about how you carry forward your own yearning for the meaning of life into the therapy space and invite your clients to join you there. We invite you to consider that these practices are spirituality.

We prefer to talk about *spirituality* in a way that separates it from religiosity. Spirituality can be a part of religion, but religion does not need to be a part of spirituality. Spirituality is instead an umbrella term to describe all aspects of meaning-making. For further clarity, we turn to Pamela Colman Smith, who reminds us that much of the power of tarot comes from its accessibility. Tarot cards are a series of images meant to evoke memories, feelings, and experiences specific to the reader or card gazer. The spirituality embodied in tarot is flexible: the cards remain the same, but the meaning you make from them is your own and cannot be dictated to you.

Spirituality comprises those Self-led practices that fill you up and give your life meaning. They need not be connected to a religious doctrine or figure. Because of the gatekeeping in the religious world, more people are drawn to spiritual traditions where they can be more autonomous, such as reading tarot cards. The cards do not discriminate between people, and there are no systems and structures in place to keep people in or out. Rather, this is a practice that one can do on their own or with others as they deem appropriate. Folks have the agency to create meaning without the dogma.

So often in therapy graduate programs, the focus is placed on cultural competency, and religion and spiritual faith get tacked on, generally as one unit within a semester-long course. But there are striking similarities between psychoanalysis and some aspects of the spiritual practice of shamanism.[6] If you have not heard that statement before, did you notice a reaction in yourself just now? Whether it was agreement, disagreement, or neutrality, pause and ponder what it means to be a therapist. Now might be a good time to jot down some of your initial reactions to these questions: Do you see therapists as spiritual healers? Do you conceive of our profession as being predominantly technical, in the sense that we teach coping skills and strategies, and we leave meaning-making to the ever-shrinking group of existential philosophers? These two poles sit on a spectrum, and it's important for you to contemplate where you fall on this continuum.

Spirituality on the Couch

Justine once had a client who was dying. While this person was able to come to terms with many aspects of the end of their life, they felt concern about not knowing what "comes after," and they felt that having an understanding of this matter could offer some comfort. This placed Justine in the position of a spiritual guide who would walk beside the dying client to help them create meaning. This person did not have a faith tradition of their own, but they believed in the power of stories. Justine worked with this client to create a narrative of what they wanted the afterlife to be. Because the client had no preconceived notions of the afterlife, they could build it in its entirety. Justine offered to them, "If nothing is true, then anything is possible."

The two cocreated an afterlife that offered the client comfort in their dying. It was difficult and important work—and it was something that none of us are trained for in therapy school. We're therapists, not theologians. While the outcome was helpful for the client, and meaningful for Justine, it was a heavy lift for her. Luckily, Justine had sages such as Thich Nhat Hanh, and the messages passed on to her by her Buddhist supervisor, to help light the way and remind her that she had wisdom inherent within her. As Thich Nhat Hanh reminds us: "What you are looking for is already in you.... You already are everything you are seeking."[7] Justine's client, while struggling, also had skills and wisdom. The two coming together on a human level and discussing meaning created an afterlife for the client.

Justine could have referred out her dying client to a spiritual advisor; but, for her, this was not the appropriate choice. In her role as guide on her client's hero's journey, she came to realize that she already occupied the role of spiritual advisor. The two had already cocreated meaning through the use of stories, and a more traditional spiritual advisor might not have been able to speak that language. She was the person for this task, and this role became part of her own therapist's hero's journey. There are things beyond scientific reasoning that connect us, and religions and spirituality have always been an attempt to, if not make sense of them, at least to give voice to those connections that exist but currently defy measurement. When Justine's client died, she grieved, but it was not a grief of despair. Rather, it was a grief honoring the life of her client and the part of the journey they took together.

Larisa has had her own unique experience with religion, spirituality, and faith in the therapy space. While not a practitioner of any religion, she has often worked with clients for whom religion, spirituality, and faith are one. One of her first clients was a born-again Christian, and God was an important part of their clinical work together. One day in supervision, Larisa's on-site supervisor asked her how she was able to incorporate God into session, to which Larisa responded: "It's just the client's favorite fandom. I involve God like I would any other important fictional character." As her work has grown and evolved, Larisa has grown in her appreciation for Gods' and Goddesses' healing power in the therapy space. She makes sense of this transformative power using the tools of Therapeutic Fanfiction, a therapeutic modality that she and Justine cocreated. This type of therapy acknowledges the very real and transformative emotional power of fictional fandom characters in a person's life.[8] Whether your God is Thor, God of thunder, or Jesus, God of the dispossessed, they are welcome in Larisa's therapy room.

As you look around the spiritual volcano in which you find yourself, we invite you to consider these questions: "Do I want to incorporate spiritual guidance into my therapy practice, or do I already do so?" You may notice a rush of feelings as you sit with this. Or you may just hear an absence—silence as you sit with the weight of such a task. You get to decide what to take from this realm of faith. And that may be the knowledge that you don't want to be a spiritual advisor to your clients and you need to compile referral resources instead. What wonderful information you're taking from this realm of myth and magic.

Perhaps you're sitting with the realization that you *do* want to incorporate spiritual awareness into your clinical work, but you're not sure how to do it, either due to training concerns or because you lack the additional energy required for this kind of work. The reality for so many full-time clinicians is that we cannot possibly do this kind of depth work with the number of clients typically expected on a fulltime caseload. Whatever you discover from your introspection, allow it to be there without judgment. Remember that you probably did not get into the therapy field to do spiritual advising (unless you're a spiritual counselor), and if this is difficult to think about, we understand. Whatever you've uncovered in your introspection, simply let it be here with you in the volcano. You can continue to get curious about it, or make a note in your journal and return when you're ready.

Grieving Tools—Reduce, Reuse, Renew

Imagine for a moment an attic in your mind. Before you in the attic is an ancient chest or trunk filled with faith messages. It's time to go through the chest and decide the fates of these messages. Which will you remove, which will you keep, which will you recreate from the spiritual or religious gifts you already have? Some of these may be ancient artifacts, some may be hand-me-down heirlooms, and some may be new gifts from a friend. Even if you cleaned out the attic of your mind long ago, there are likely still items in the chest that you set aside to decide on later.

This is how we can conceive of our deconstruction of faith. For thousands of years, human beings have created narratives and objects to represent powerful emotions, memories, and people. These stories and totems can evoke healing processes, but they can also overtake us and become distractions from facing the reality of existence. Using the grieving tools of distraction and denial, we will explore how stories and totems can be used either as tools for healing and deeper connection or as buffers from reality, fostering avoidance and division rather than honest confrontation and healing collaboration. This grieving tool invites you to recontextualize a part of your former faith tradition that you once found meaningful by creating or finding a physical object. This talisman, if you will, can serve as a concrete reminder of the parts of your current spirituality that you have already integrated or are currently in the process of integrating into your present story of meaning.

Clients

Regardless of where your client is on the journey of deconstructing their faith tradition, it's helpful throughout this process to invite clients to hold on to those traditions, rituals, or physical objects from their faith that continue to have positive meaning-making properties for them. Like all stories, there is emotional truth and purposeful meaning to be found in every religious faith. Strange as it is to write this sentence, there is even emotional truth in QAnon. Sex trafficking—one of the QAnon movement's chief obsessions—is an abhorrent reality that is created and maintained by the upper class of America and many other countries. However, religions often become problematic when their systemic structure solidifies into rigidity. Rigor mortis! Meaning-making, the sixth stage of grief, reminds us of the importance of meaning-making in healing. Helping your clients to sift through the harmful systemic oppression and find the narrative jewels of meaning that perhaps once brought them to this faith tradition can paradoxically help them to pass back those oppressive parts and keep the meaningful story.

Larisa once had a client who once considered themselves a member of the Catholic faith. For this client, rosary beads were a frequent topic of discussion. As a former member of the Church, they expressed feeling torn about the "Christness" of the beads and the positive experiences they remembered having with the beads during quiet prayer and contemplation. Larisa invited the client to approach the rosary as they might any other mindfulness object, explaining that they need not pass back every part of their previous tradition. Over time, the client came to see their rosary as a meaningful personal artifact—one that did not belong to the Catholic Church. In their repurposing of the beads from rosary to meditation tool, the client kept the aspects of their Catholic experience they still cherished and passed back those aspects that no longer served them.

Therapist

We know that the Realm of Our Faith has been a journey. But we also invite you to take a look through the faith trunk that you have in the attic of your mind. Open it up and explore what's inside. Is it full of old things that no longer serve you? Or have you already been through here a time or two (or ten) and pulled things out to pass along as gifts at the ephemeral donation station? Take stock of what's here without assigning any judgment to what you find, or to yourself. You are right where you need to be right now.

As you observe what's in the trunk, just sit with the feelings for a moment. Notice if feelings of judgment want to come up. Whatever feelings arise come from parts that have feelings about what is in the trunk, and they're trying to protect you from having to deal with them. Let those parts know that you see them and that you know they're trying to help. Now ask if they will just hang back and be with you while you go through the trunk. They can speak up at any time if it gets too upsetting. But you can always remind them that you're a grown-up who can handle tough things.

As you handle each item, take a moment to check in with yourself, Marie Kondo style. Does this item spark joy? No? Then thank it for its service and send it to the ephemeral donation station. Or you can set it aside for upcycling, or place it in the closet of your active mind. It doesn't need to live in a trunk anymore. It's part of you, and it gets to be with you out here, not hidden in there.

Due North: Self of the Therapist

Consider for a moment your own spiritual or meaning-making practice. Remember that this practice need not be religious; rather, it's what you're doing in your life that offers meaning and an opportunity for nurturance and growth. For us, the authors, stories are how we make sense of the world. Engaging with stories—be they books, movies, or video games—offers us the opportunity to engage with modern mythology and tap into the ancient power of archetypes to aid in our own healing. In a way, fandom is a polytheistic spiritual practice for us.

If, when you consider your own meaning-making practice, you find that you aren't fulfilled by it, or that there's nothing really there when you look, this is valuable information. It's simply an invitation for further introspection. Some of the most powerful meaning-making comes from stories (and not just religious mythology, as we mentioned above), but another way is through our engagement with nature. How often are you in relation to the four elements? For both of your authors, water is another impactful part of spiritual practice. Justine and Larisa both live near water—Justine in Minneapolis, and Larisa in Chicago. Being able to access this precious resource regularly via long walks is healing for both. Water invites us to reflect on ourselves, just as water reflects what is before it.

We, the authors, do not attempt to convert clients to our particular spiritual practice. That would be neither ethical nor appropriate. But having our own meaning-making practice with which we engage on a daily basis gives us a framework to use with our clients. While the details of our beliefs differ, we conceive of all spiritual practices as being founded on the following principles: community, mindfulness, meaning-making, structure for understanding the natural world (including our own mortality), and purpose in what feels like a chaotic universe. So even if you don't ascribe to any particular faith tradition, how do you attempt to get these needs met in your own life? For instance, perhaps these needs are met for you through attending fitness classes or joining a book club. All of your needs will likely not be met by just one group or activity. This is where it may be helpful to consider spending time with your new friend Thich Nhat Hanh. While he is clearly from the Buddhist tradition, his books are made for laypeople, and they offer the opportunity to take what works for you and leave the rest.

You don't need to fully commit to a faith tradition. If you're an atheist, fear not. God need not be involved in your spiritual practice. But curiosity and a willingness to practice holding space for the ephemeral and phenomenological will help deepen your connection with the natural world and your ability to hold compassionate space with clients as they explore meaning-making.

Due West: Supervision

If you're a supervisee with an interest in learning ways to incorporate spiritual presence into your therapy, it may be worthwhile for you to seek out a supervisor who can help you build this skill set. Be cautious of supervisors who attempt to convince or cajole you into specific details of a spiritual approach. It's often most helpful to work with a supervisor who gets curious with you about your own experience of the spiritual and the infinite, and who then helps you explore ways to integrate this experience into your clinical work. Conversely, if you find that your supervisor is trying to convince you to use their style of spirituality, either in the therapy room or in your own life, and this is not something you want, be sure to let your supervisor know. If they persist, find another supervisor.

Supervisors, you can play an instrumental role in helping supervisees both practice and prepare for the spiritual aspect of counseling and therapy. By sharing your own spiritual practice and how you incorporate this praxis into your therapeutic and personal work, you help supervisees learn the structure of spirituality. The focus here is not at all on converting and instead is all about the power of social modeling. During their training in therapy graduate school, Larisa and Justine both trained under a supervisor who was a practicing Buddhist and a devotee of ayurvedic (yogic) medicine. Their supervisor brought the teachings of mindfulness, sacred presence, and deep compassion into group supervision. Because spirituality was so integrated into this supervisor's approach, neither Larisa nor Justine felt as though she was pushing any sort of religious agenda or asking supervisees to believe in a particular deity or dogma. The supervisor's spirituality was simply another aspect of her therapeutic and supervisory presence, and the authors could appreciate the gifts she brought into the room without knowing exactly from whence they came.

So, supervisors, don't be afraid to show up as your whole, authentic self in the supervisory space. Be curious with supervisees about what self-of-the-therapist needs they have around meaning-making, and whether they need or want support around spiritual concerns in the therapy room.

Due East: Education

"Psych is not enough." This is the title of a slide that Justine shows her graduate school class each semester. The slide enumerates a number of different types of knowledge, including disciplinary, interdisciplinary, and Indigenous. It's not enough for therapists to know about psychology, because humans are more than their psychology. In fact, people also contain an awful lot of philosophy. Often this slide produces some anxiety for her students, who may exclaim, "I don't know Kierkegaard!" Students reading this book, it's okay if you, too, do not know Kierkegaard. You don't need to know major thinkers in philosophy (although it might help, depending upon your and your clients' interests), but knowing something about the existential questions that drive humans is invaluable: Why are we here? What happens after we die? All humans grapple with these questions.

Historically, the practice of religion has been one of the main ways that people answer these questions. While we often conceive of religion as a set of ancient communal rituals passed down through the ages, humans have also created new religious myths and rites as part of how they processed and made sense of catastrophic events, like plagues, and more personal events, like the death of a child. If you're not getting information about the importance of various types of knowledge in your graduate school classes, be sure to ask for this information or seek it out yourself. You can approach your professors or school directors to ask them to share more information with you. If they're unwilling or unable, check out some of the resources listed at the end of this book.

Teachers, it is also okay for you not to know Kierkegaard, but we invite you to let your students know there is more to this work than just psychology. Even if topics outside psychology are not the work they *want* to do, it's certainly the work they *will* do, so best to set them up for success with some information on the front end. Clients manifest spirituality in a variety of ways, and if students are to support their clients, the students' worldview must be varied as well. If this is new to you, that makes sense. You likely did not get into teaching graduate counseling students in order to teach about philosophy, and we're not asking you to become proficient in religion and philosophy. We're simply inviting you to make your students aware that if they hope to help clients make meaning, they need to understand more about the world than just what's inside their psychotherapy textbooks.

Due South: Death and Love

A spiritual practice is one of the core ways that human beings attempt to understand and dwell within—which is to say, to be present with—death and love. The reality of our work as therapists is that we'll be called upon to face death with our clients. Even if we refer out to a specific spiritual advisor, we must learn how to make space for death in the therapy room. This means we must learn how to sit with death as individual human beings.

In the Realm of Our Faith, alone inside a dead volcano, you may be reminded of one of the oldest truths about existence: we each have our own personal relationship with death. All deaths are singular experiences, and no two are alike. The stories we tell ourselves about our lives, our communities, and our purpose help us prepare for those final moments when everything falls away and we face our own personal end. Spirituality encompasses all that we do to make meaning in this life and prepare for that final conversation with death.

As you look around the walls of the inactive volcano depicting the many ways that humans before you have attempted to make sense of life and death, you take out your map and reflect on those stories that bring you back to your meaning and purpose. You decide to do a rubbing of some of the etchings on the volcano walls. You dig a piece of charcoal out of your rucksack, and as you move your charcoal across the paper, you realize that the silence that surrounds you no longer feels frightening or grim. Instead, the silence feels familiar, like an old friend with whom you can sit in companionable silence.

8

THE REALM OF OUR CRISIS

If we can accept where we are, and not judge the disruption in our life as wrong or bad, we can touch freedom. This is because fighting what is doesn't actually work.
—KAIRA JEWEL LINGO[1]

Before you consider how you're going to get out of this volcano, we welcome a new sage. Kaira Jewel Lingo is a former Buddhist nun who studied at the knee of Thich Nhat Hanh. Kaira describes herself as having grown up "in an interracial family within an ecumenical Christian order." In her forties she realized that the monastic life was no longer her calling, and she has since rejoined society.[2] Kaira went through many internal struggles to make her choice and come to terms with the new world she was entering. The daughter of a preacher who marched with Dr. Martin Luther King Jr., Kaira is an ideal guide through the Realm of Our Crisis. She has witnessed both calm and chaos, and she has much to teach us about how to move through our crises with humility.

You take a deep breath and look around you. The cavernous depths of the volcano seem darker than before and as you look up to the distant opening in the volcano, you see the barest outline of a crescent moon's shadow. How long have you been in this volcano? You shiver and begin to gather up your items, shoving them into your rucksack. Before you get up, you pull a thick sweater from your pack. It feels pleasantly nubbly under your fingertips and soft with nary a scratch as you pull it over your head. As you stand, you look around and attempt to scout a way out of this place. Climbing back up the way you came feels impossible. So high and steep with no one to assist you. To your right you see nothing but magma. To your left, you notice a tunnel.

You decide to try your luck in the tunnel. Your headlamp's light is a steady beacon as you step into the passage. It's nearly tall enough for you, so you just barely stoop as you make your way forward. You sigh—relieved that this is not one of those low-ceilinged tunnels that requires total hunching or crawling. While you aren't opposed to indoor spaces, tight, dimly lit spaces definitely are not your idea of a good time.

Perhaps you judged too soon. You're barely ten meters into the hike when you notice that the ceiling seems to be getting lower with every step. As you continue walking, you hear the sound of your pack brushing against the ceiling and now the walls. Are the walls narrowing? You attempt to ignore mental images of tight spaces and crawling bugs as you move ever deeper into the tunnel. Your headlamp flickers—stutters.

The light goes out. Your chest tightens. You release a series of colorful expletives that bounce off the tunnel's walls. For a moment you consider turning back; but you can't even turn your body around. You try to steady your breathing as you cross your arms in an attempt to make yourself even smaller as you winnow your way through the tunnel. There isn't even enough space to take off your pack, and even if you could, finding the extra set of batteries you packed would be slow going without a light to guide you. Finally you kneel down and begin to crawl through what feels like damp sand—the darkness closing in.

Then you hear it—a soft whistling sound from up ahead. Could it be an opening in this seemingly endless tunnel? You take another breath and blow it out for a count of four as you continue to crawl toward the whistling sound, which is soon accompanied by the sensation of cold air. Yes, it has to be an opening!

You muscle your way toward the sound, willing yourself forward with the promise of a gasp of fresh air. Finally you tumble out of the tunnel onto lush grass. You fill your lungs with the sweetest air you could imagine and lie down completely exhausted in the cool predawn. You hear the whistling sound again, and realize it wasn't just the wind. No, the whistle was a bird call. Its trill continues as you shrug and stretch your stiff limbs.

Yawning, you stand up and head toward what seems like a path, squinting fiercely to try to make out the shades of deep grays, blues, and blacks filling your field of vision. The birdsong stops, and you hear the sound of beating wings, but before you can duck, bird claws hit the back of your head. You cry out, nearly pitching forward, but then you sharply veer right because the bird is swooping back around for another attack on your left. Covering your head with your hands, you attempt to stay as far to the right as you can as you run from this wild bird. At that moment the sun finally lifts above the horizon. You notice the mountain wall to your right and realize you've run several steps now without the bird attacking. You stop running and bend over with your hands on your knees. With a flutter of wings, a blackbird alights just a yard up the path and cocks its head at you. The bird ruffles its feathers and begins to preen its right wing—a deep ebony with a scarlet center.

You say to the bird, "What was that all about?" You glance back toward where you came and see that the tunnel empties out very near to a steep cliff. You might have walked right off the edge if the red-winged blackbird hadn't herded you to safety. Suddenly the dull throbbing in the back of your head provokes a feeling other than anger. You look with softened feelings toward the bird, but they're no longer perched before you. Instead, they're flying at you again, whirling around you, making you dizzy.

Panic! In the Therapy Room

We have all felt panic, whether it was the panic of your very first client sitting in front of you, or the first time a client endorsed suicidality. Sometimes the physical and cognitive symptoms of panic are strong indicators that we're in the middle of a crisis; but, perhaps just as often, they're simply indicators that our nervous system is responding incongruously. And then there are the types of panic we experience in our lives outside the therapy room. They impact our work, but they are not of the work. These are the panics we feel about loved ones who are sick or lost, or in response to other dangers in our life that we can't control. Many of us experienced panic in the early days of the COVID-19 pandemic. Little was known about the virus—only that it was transmissible and deadly. Pause for a moment, and if it's tolerable, remember your panic. Feel that panic in your body for a moment. Remember how you managed that panic, or how you struggled to manage it. For these authors, we threw ourselves into our work. We set about calming the panic of our clients, and we exhausted ourselves.

Just like the Spanish Inquisition, nobody expects a crisis. And yet, we all want to be prepared for any possible scenario. Justine has this conversation with students often. Students want to be prepared for every possible occurrence, no matter how unlikely, but even the ever-inquisitive graduate students couldn't have predicted a pandemic. It can be hard to know that it's impossible to be prepared for every situation. Justine helps students learn how to feel some of the feelings that come up in that sort of situation through experiential role-plays, and through some intentional provocation to evoke an emotional response. It's not a perfect facsimile, but at least it's an approximation to help prepare for future calamity.

When you're in the early stages of a crisis, the most important thing is to get yourself to a place of physical and emotional safety. From there, you can figure out next steps and a plan. Often in the clinical realm, getting to this safe space of reprieve requires us to be honest with ourselves about the extent of the crisis. We sometimes get the message that we need to remain focused on the client and compartmentalize our own internal pain to be dealt with later. But in the realm of crisis, you may not be able to attend to your Internal Family System in the ways that it requires while still supporting your clients. When you're emotionally flooded, you cannot and should not meet with a client. Signs of being emotionally flooded include the sudden inability to focus, dissociating, "seeing red" or any other single color, sudden intense ringing or roaring in your ears, sudden hot or cold sweats, difficulty in breathing, numbness in one or more of your physical extremities, or an overwhelming feeling of "I just can't." The reality is that any of these symptoms coupled with an inciting incident of crisis are enough of a reason to cancel part or all of the rest of your clinical day. If that feels like a hard message, we hear you. And we gently remind you that our first ethical obligation to our clients is to do no harm (i.e., ahimsa). When we sit down for a therapy session in a state of internal overwhelm, we're putting our clients at risk of harm perpetrated by us.

You might be thinking, "But maybe I could still help someone!" Of course you want that to be true. And while it's possible that you might be able to help someone, what's true is that you'll definitely be hurting yourself. Remember that ahimsa extends to ourselves as well.

When you appear overwhelmed, distracted, or in pain in a session, you're showing your clients that you do not believe yourself worthy of care. Thus, the message your clients might receive is that *they* are not worthy of care. Remember that we're modeling for our clients how to show up for themselves in the world. If you're struggling with the idea of canceling one or more sessions for the day due to your own sudden crisis, ask yourself: "Do I want to model self-sacrifice—which is to say, self-harming behavior—for my client?" We realize that sometimes these decisions are not just about wanting to show up for clients; we could also be motivated by financial reasons or fear of retaliation by an employer. We recognize that these are realities. It is also no less real that you are a vital human who deserves to care for yourself and your loved ones in a time of crisis.

Crises tend to come in two forms: collective and individual. These can, of course, overlap or combine to varying degrees. We have all experienced individual crises: a loved one is sick or dying, a car accident, or emergency surgery. And we have now all experienced collective crises: mass shootings, war, bombings, and police violence, to name just a few. But for some folks, collective trauma taps into historical traumas that compound the impact of those events. For the BIPOC community, the murder of Mr. George Floyd by police is one of many examples of such violence perpetrated against the bodies of Black and Brown people. And while folks who are not people of color were experiencing the collective trauma of that event, folks of color experienced this as an additional layer of collective trauma on top of the collective trauma events that have been happening since the beginning of colonialism. We're all impacted, but we're impacted differently based on our lived experiences and intersectional identities. Justine, as a Minneapolis resident, had a front seat to the trauma that occurred in her community. As a white woman, her experience differed from those of her neighbors of color. This was something for her to keep in mind as a clinician: everyone is hurting or experiencing anger, but not all in the same way.

Kaira invites us to recognize that all those who are suffering need compassion and for those who are less impacted to listen, allowing those who are more impacted to express their emotions. She offers a way to engage with these emotions, similar to Internal Family Systems work:

> Once mindfulness recognizes anger, it begins to accept it and give it space. We open to our experience of anger and allow it to be here. We generate compassion for ourselves, recognizing anger is a part of us so we don't want to reject or judge it. However, accepting anger doesn't mean we give it freedom to cause destruction. Mindfulness is there with it in the living room, so it can do no harm. When we've accepted it, we embrace it.... We hold it, rock it, soothe it. We can even speak to this part of ourselves as we practice saying, "My dear anger, I'm here for you."[3]

Let us return to the mountain path and the red-winged blackbird full of hard messages. The bird's swooping and dive bombing continues unabated until you hear a loud crash coming from several yards ahead of you. As rocks begin to fall down the mountain, you and the red-winged blackbird dive for cover behind a large boulder. You bump your head on the rock and see stars. When the thundering sounds stop, you and the red-winged blackbird slowly and cautiously peer over the top of the boulder and stare directly into two large golden eyes. You jump back and stare up into the face of a giant furry creature. Could this be—a forest yeti?!

The red-winged blackbird soars upward, but before it can even attempt to dive-bomb the forest yeti, the yeti gently reaches out a giant bark-hued paw and scoops up the bird. You watch spellbound as the yeti lifts her other paw and begins to gently pat the red-winged blackbird's head. At first, the bird struggles; but then, the forest yeti begins to sing. Shifting back and forth in a steady rhythm that causes the ground underneath you to faintly rumble, you find your own breathing matching the steady rhythm of her song. You watch as the red-winged blackbird's eyes begin to close, realizing that the corners of your own eyes are beginning to soften. The forest yeti takes such care of the red-winged blackbird, and you think that perhaps you were too harsh with it. It did hurt to get dive-bombed like that, but the bird was just doing what it could to make sure you didn't plunge off the side of that cliff. It meant well and just did not have the skills to react with anything other than aggressive alarm.

Crisis Management

How do you cope with the crisis at hand? Let's begin with sitting down with the grief and sadness that often come with personal crises. As clinicians, we frequently deal with client crises, and it can feel profoundly unfair when we're faced with our own crises, too. It's also fairly common for clinicians to lean into work in response to crises; that is, they lean into supporting their clients through crisis as a way to avoid facing the crises bubbling up in their own personal lives. This is understandable. In our roles as therapists, we feel competent and capable. We know we have the skills with which to face crises that don't directly impact us. But when it comes to ourselves, we are no longer in the position of a witness to a crisis. Instead, we're a player in the crisis. If this resonates for you, we invite you to take some time to acknowledge and hold space for the loss of both competence and control that we all experience when we cease to be witnesses and become victims of it.

    Once you start to be present with your own feelings, the time has come to begin formulating a plan that will help you move through this crisis. Depending on the severity of the crisis, you may need to take some or a lot of time away from your job as a clinician. You may need to reach out not just to your employer but also to friends and colleagues who can help you figure out the details of a leave, such as how to explain your absence to your clients and how much time to take off from work. Most of all, you must come to terms with what you're capable of doing and what's not possible for you to do during this time. You've been handed a new set of limitations (see chapter 2), and you must now find ways to get creative within these limitations.

These new limitations bring with them their own special kind of grief as you face the way you once worked, and as you let go of this chosen path, because life has forced you onto a different road. Some of these roads will lead you down a new path entirely or change your work for the rest of your career. Take a moment to sit with the reality that your path has changed, perhaps permanently, because of this event. This total loss of control can feel both terrifying and miserable. Like the red-winged blackbird, you may need to find your own forest yeti who can help you start to calm and face the new realities of your existence.

One of the more complicated experiences we face as clinicians is when we're caught up in the same crisis as our clients. Certainly, this happened during the initial phase of the COVID-19 pandemic. It also happens during acts of violence such as mass shootings, police brutality, war, and bombings. During these crises, you will likely need to reach out for immediate consultation to help you determine what, if anything, you can do for your clients.

It can be especially hard if we see situations differently from our clients or coworkers. One of the areas where we've seen this show up is around mass shooting events. The perpetrators of these crimes are overwhelmingly white folks who make it out of the events alive, unless they choose "suicide by cop." Often these shootings are in suburban areas where these types of events are locally processed by both press and community as uncommon, and they cause outrage. Whereas in the city, similar acts of violence tend to be processed by both press and community as omnipresent. These intersections of different perspectives and experiences further complicate instances where individual and collective crises collide.

If you've experienced these kinds of collisions, you already know how emotionally fraught and exhausting they can be. If you haven't experienced this, we invite you to consider for a moment the feelings that come up for you as you sit with this challenging hypothetical. Once these events enter the therapy room or coworker space, you have a few choices: you can ignore it, call folks "in," or address it in some other way. Much of this will depend on your style of therapy and how much of your Self you bring into the therapy room.

When it comes to colleagues and coworkers, we encourage you to share only what truly feels safe to share. *Call-ins* assume neutral to positive intent on the other person's part; they invite the other person to consider whether they've thought about a situation from a different angle, and they offer the perspective of other parties involved. All of this is done kindly and in good faith. In contrast, *call-outs* criticize the other person and are rarely successful in changing folks' minds or getting them to consider alternative points of view. We invite you to consider that call-ins require a great deal of emotional energy and emotional labor. If you're in the midst of navigating a crisis, that's likely not the time for you to call-in anyone except your Internal Family System. Remember Kaira's invitation to recognize those parts that are hurting and to "embrace" them with "kindness and concern."[4]

Memento Mori

In Kaira's Buddhist tradition, they practice the "five remembrances," a contemplation on five thoughts each day: "that we are of the nature to grow old, to have ill health, and to die, that our loved ones are of the nature to change and we can't avoid being separated from them, and lastly, that our actions are our only true possessions, we don't get to take anything else with us when we pass away."[5] While this may feel grim, the purpose is to focus the mind on the concept of impermanence and to appreciate even more what we have right now in this very moment. This can be a valuable remembrance when we're going through a crisis. First, it reminds us that whatever is happening right now is not permanent, as everything in this life will change. It's the only thing we can be sure of in this life. Second, this practice helps us foster moments of gratitude for what's still going well in our lives at this moment, even though the crisis may feel overwhelming. While the five remembrances are a part of the Buddhist tradition, we can find similar meditations and rituals on death across religious and spiritual traditions.[6]

Crisis causes a shock to our nervous systems. Particularly when we're experiencing a new type of crisis for which we have little to no experience or coping strategy, we can dissociate rather than staying present and figuring out how to respond. In such moments, it's valuable to have language available to help anchor you safely in the moment. Remembering our own mortality, and that of others, offers this language. The language affirms the gravity of the crisis while also reminding humans that they're not alone in this crisis—you have suffered before and you will suffer again. Although modern societies often focus on the unfairness of a crisis, Kaira reminds us that this, too, is a fundamental part of being alive. While this is a hard message, it can be a grounding message as it validates the horrific aspects of your crisis and reminds you that you stand in solidarity with all life in facing struggle.

Grieving Tools—Mirror, Mirror

Social modeling can be a powerful tool both inside and outside of the therapy space. We don't necessarily recommend using this tool when you're grappling with your own personal crisis and taking time away from work to care for yourself. Rather, this is a tool that can help you as you move through the grief that inevitably follows a time of crisis. You can use the tool of social modeling as you navigate your personal struggles outside of session as well as exploring the use of this tool with clients inside the therapy space.

Consider for a moment clients with whom you've worked who struggle with emotional expression. As a trained clinician, you can tell when they're feeling sad, even when their affect is incongruent with sadness. The "mirror, mirror" tool offers you a simple intervention in such circumstances: you can literally demonstrate, via your facial expressions, vocal inflection, and language ways to congruently express sadness. You can act out what different feelings look like, as well as modeling emotionally congruent reactions to what another person shares. In this way, clients get the opportunity to see and be seen as fully human, and practice ways to express their feelings.

Client

The "mirror, mirror" tool allows us to harness the power of mirror neurons to help us guide our clients toward understanding through modeling. Mirror neurons are the parts of our brain that make us feel like we are experiencing what we observe someone else doing. This feeling can thus motivate us to mimic this observed behavior. So, for instance, when our client sees us setting boundaries and respecting ourselves and our time and autonomy and recognizing when we need a break, their mirror neurons fire and then they start to emotionally experience what it would be like if they did the same. Who do you mirror? Or rather, who is your mirror? We are an infinite mirror reflection. Imagine standing in the bathroom between two mirrors and seeing them reflect each other ad infinitum; that is what we do. We learn from what was mirrored to us, and we teach what we mirror to others, and so on, and so on. Consider what you're mirroring and what you're presenting to be mirrored.

Whether or not you decide to disclose the nature of the crisis you experienced or the pain you're feeling afterward, how you interact with your client around it gives the client important messages. If you decide to disclose appropriately, sharing brief details from a place of emotional presence but not overwhelm, you're teaching that it's okay for people to go through hard things—even people who seem to have it all together (as clients usually think their therapists do). If you decide not to disclose but rather to set boundaries and let clients know your limitations, you're modeling how to express what you need without apologizing for being a person.

Therapist

Those drawn to the therapy field can often readily think of experiences when their pain was overwhelming and either a therapist or a guide helped them face this pain and move forward. Ironically, the longer we work in the field as therapists, the more challenging it can be to return to that place where we are the ones in pain and in need of help. When we ourselves are grieving, it's harder to find mirrors to reflect back what we need. So many of our loved ones are in their own pain, and that can be hard to stand in front of and witness. And yet, we invite you to allow the pain of others to become part of your mirror experience. We have to grieve together. Experience the pain of those around you, and notice what it prompts inside you. Some of those around you will be in various stages of grief, and you can give yourself permission to experience and reflect back on all the stages, feeling it all and letting it become a part of you.

After years of using the "mirror, mirror" tool in session with her clients, Justine has recently begun to observe them using the tool without prompting—even within the therapeutic relationship. For years she has modeled for clients the importance of them taking care of themselves, whether by eating a sandwich during session or canceling because they don't feel well. She ends each session by saying "take good care of you." She now finds that her clients regularly tell her to "take care" when she's sick, and they affirm to her that she must "take care of" herself so she "can show up" for them. What Justine's clients have learned by watching her and experiencing her as their therapist is that we must come through for ourselves first before we can help others.

Due North: Self of the Therapist

So you're in crisis and feeling overwhelmed with panic. What do you do? Well, first you need to assess the rest of your day. If you have clients scheduled or supervisees with whom to meet, the hard message here is that you just cannot meet with them. The first time you have to cancel due to an emergency will probably sting a little bit. You might have guilt or shame with which to contend. But you must remember that going into therapy when you're emotionally compromised doesn't help anyone. In fact, it means you're putting yourself in a position to potentially do harm to your client, and you're definitely causing yourself harm.

While Larisa was working as an in-home family therapist, she once was involved in a car accident on her way to a client session. It was snowing in the middle of a Minnesota winter, and she was sideswiped. Her car spun a full 180 degrees across the highway. When she was finally able to stop her vehicle, she was badly shaken emotionally and in the early stages of severe pain. At the time, she was working for a terrible organization that offered no paid medical leave, and, as you might expect, paid her below minimum wage. This is all too common for preclinical folks. Larisa sat in her car on the side of the highway and asked herself: "What can I do?" As she took some shaky breaths, she realized that she was neither physically nor emotionally capable of meeting with her clients that day. Instead, she took a few more moments and then restarted her car to drive to a safer area so she could make the necessary phone calls, first to her partner and then to her clients to cancel the remainder of her workday.

Before you ask, Larisa was unable to file for worker's compensation because she had signed a contract releasing her employer from any liability for injuries she sustained due to driving to do in-home family therapy. Are you angry? So are we. Bottom line, Larisa knew she could not do effective therapy that day. Even though she knew there would be financial consequences to not meeting with her clients, she felt that it would be unsafe for her to go to work. And trust us, at the time, she would go to work even when work was literally killing her via black mold. So, high bar.

Once you've begun to radically accept that you can't proceed with your work day, we invite you to reach out to a trusted friend. Just like the red-winged blackbird, you might need a forest yeti to offer you comfort and calm support. Who comes to mind for you? It might be a colleague or a best friend. It might be a partner or your best cat, Katsu. Whoever comes to mind, you might just take a moment to acknowledge that they will be there for you to help you do the emotional processing you'll need to do.

Depending upon what order feels best, you might reach out to this person before you cancel with your clients, or you might reach out to your clients first. Regardless of the order, we invite you to be brief but clear in your communication, because you likely will not have the emotional energy or capacity to do the more in-depth therapeutic modeling that can happen when you're ready to return to work. For now, letting your clients know you have a personal emergency and telling them whom they can reach out to in case of their own clinical emergency is all you need to do. You don't owe them the reasoning for your absence. Some clients and even employers will ask you to explain the nature of the emergency. You don't need to tell them, and in some cases it would be ill advised to do so.

While Justine was still in her preclinical practice, she underwent a major surgical procedure, and her supervisor advised her not to share that this was the reason for her absence. The supervisor feared clients would become distressed and want to care-take. In this case, Justine had a hysterectomy to deal with debilitating endometriosis. She had not intended to tell clients the exact surgery she was having, but she did think it made sense to let them know she would be undergoing surgery. Justine's supervisor, however, cautioned that either way clients were likely to have a reaction to the news that their therapist was undergoing surgery and be concerned for her well-being, perhaps to their own detriment.

Today, many years later, Justine understands her supervisor's warnings, but now that appropriate self-disclosure is an integral part of her practice, she would use this information therapeutically with clients to help them navigate what it's like when someone that you care about has to deal with something difficult. This is an opportunity to name and model boundaries around care and concern. Now, when Justine shares a bit more about why she's suddenly taking time away from her practice (as she did recently when she contracted COVID-19), her clients understand that they don't need to take care of her. They do need to respect her need to care for herself. And they have a model of how to do this in their own lives, thanks to the way Justine has modeled it for them. This example shows that it's a clinical judgment call. So think about how much you want to share, why you want to share it, and what impact it could have.

Due West: Supervision

Historically, taking time away due to a personal crisis is very challenging for supervisees who are new to this work. They become easily overwhelmed by the fear of having this conversation and being seen as too weak to be in the field. We've had this conversation with many supervisees who are fearful of talking with their site supervisors about anything that causes them to appear to have human fallibility. And we tell them: that fear is not theirs to hold. If they feel that their employer or site supervisor will think badly of them for being a person, then that supervisor or employer has not given the supervisee permission to be a person. Remember, supervisees, you are people, and people have problems. In the immortal words of Michael White, the cofounder of narrative therapy and map aficionado, a person is not a problem; a problem is a problem. If your site supervisor/employer won't respect your human needs, then that's valuable information you have just learned about them.

Supervisors must take responsibility for initiating preparatory conversations with their supervisees around the topic of crisis before a crisis occurs. When you're in these leadership roles, you have the opportunity to be the change you want to see in the field, meaning that you can help normalize that therapists are humans and sometimes need to take time to care for themselves and their family members. We need not be Nietzschean superhumans; it's enough to be our fallible selves. Having a written action plan for supervisees to reference when they're either in a state of crisis or helping a colleague through a crisis can be incredibly helpful. And please remember that you, too, are human, so remember to model your human needs for your supervisees, including canceling with them when you experience a crisis.

Due East: Education

Hello, students. Sit back and let us tell you a tale—a tale of having to manage crises of both the individual and collective variety while you're in graduate school. For Justine, this looked like letting professors know that her father-in-law was dying and that she needed to leave the state. She had to ask for some accommodations so she could get work done remotely and send it in while she was gone. At the time, she felt that this was important enough that she should be offered these accommodations. Justine was also in her thirties and had returned to school for a second career. She knew how to advocate for herself and to call-in those in power if they failed to respect her wishes. If you're a younger person who wants to impress your professors, you still get to ask for accommodations.

Also, students, the world is changing all around you so quickly. The news is lit up like a fireball every night and all day on social media. There's always a collective crisis to which you can respond. Some of them will feel more important than others, but they all feel like a call to action. We invite you to remember that you cannot solve all of the world's problems, nor can you feel the pain of all the world's hurt. Remember that simply deciding to become part of the healing profession means you're on the side of the helpers. If folks in your cohort are having difficulty around a certain event and are inviting you to panic with them, pause. Remember that this person is not intending to cause you harm; they simply don't know how to hold this distress. You get to set boundaries and let your cohort member know why you're putting that boundary in place.

Teachers, you might find that many more students are getting accommodations now than in the "olden days." And you might find a feeling coming up around that. We invite you to consider all of the crises that those who are in graduate school now have had to face as part of the collective, let alone what they may be facing in their own lives. Please give respect to accommodations and honor them. Please do not make students reach out to you and ask you to offer reasonable accommodations that they have been granted by the school's disability services office. Teachers are modeling for their therapy students how to show up in the world of therapists, so let's start them off on the path of being heard and seen and respected in the hope that the next generation of clinicians can help support this panicking world that has been created for them.

We also want to invite you to be mindful of your own experience of personal and collective crises. It's okay for you to take time off, and depending on your level of comfort, it's also okay for you to name for your students what's going on with you. When it comes to collective crises, we invite you to be mindful of which crises you bring up in class and which you don't. When the Ukraine–Russian war broke out in 2022, Justine had strong feelings about the issue and felt it was important to bring this up in class. What she discovered was that it was helpful for some students, especially those of Ukrainian heritage. But it felt marginalizing to students of color who felt that wars in African countries are often overlooked, and they didn't appreciate the media narrative that was prevalent at the time: "Ukrainians, they're just like us (i.e., white America)." This was of course not Justine's intention, but it was a valuable piece of learning. Our invitation to you is to talk through events like this with a trusted colleague to decide whether this is an event to bring into class, or whether this is something you need to spend some time on in your own therapy and with your Internal Family System before you're ready to facilitate a classroom dialogue.

Due South: Death and Love

The forest yeti, the red-winged blackbird, and you sit in a circle. You can't tell if the red-winged blackbird is awake, asleep, or simply in a deeply meditative state, since it hasn't yet opened its eyes. The forest yeti is still faintly singing her song as you take your journal out of your rucksack and flip to an open page. You start drafting a sketch of this realm of panic, and as you do, you occasionally glance up and notice that the yeti is watching your pencil as it moves across the page. You pause and begin to sketch a drawing of the forest yeti, moving in short strokes to simply capture the essence rather than the details of this giant, peaceful creature. When you've finished, you hold up the journal for the forest yeti to see. You smile as the forest yeti stops singing and instead begins to laugh—a low reverberation that might be confused for a growl if not for the smile that accompanies it.

Crisis and the intense emotions that ensue have the power to drastically change our lives, sweeping away many carefully laid plans and projects. The loss of these things can be devastating; we invest so much of ourselves into the things we build. If you have experienced or are experiencing a sudden tragic loss, we invite you to be present with all of the sadness, anger, confusion, and terror that comes. You'll likely need help and support being with these feelings. But as you've probably already guessed, being present with the emotions of loss tells you what you might want to re-create or at least try to find again in this new postcrisis existence. When crisis takes from us something we love, we need not give it up forever. We mourn, and through this mourning we try to find a way to bring parts of that love into the present.

9

THE REALM OF OUR INDUSTRY

> *In the beginning, we were all psychotherapists. And it was good.*
> —BRUCE MINOR, MINNESOTA MEMBER OF THE MFT COMMUNITY[1]

The time has come to face our industry and sit with the ways the therapy system in which we work helps us, hurts us, and holds us to a standard impossible to meet. Throughout this book we have touched on many issues facing our work; now we are looking specifically at the system in which we work. No longer a collection of individual practitioners who see each other as fellow members of a therapeutic federation, our industry has become compartmentalized, industrialized, and controlled by third-party payers.

As you begin this leg of the journey, we invite you to pause and reflect on the mentors and experiences who supported you on your quest to become a therapist. We welcome you to reflect on mentors of both the past and the present as well as those with whom you had a challenging or even fraught relationship. Even those mentors and supervisors who we experience as awful can teach us valuable lessons (though that does not exonerate them).

When it comes to mentors and supervisors, we, the authors, have had the best and the worst. For this chapter, we reflect on some of the greats from our local MFT community: Anne Ramage, PsyD, LMFT, our graduate school professor who taught us so much more than we ever realized there was to know about Carl Whitaker; and the collective of marriage and family therapists who have sustained the Minnesota field for decades, some of whom also became our supervisors and mentors: Ginny D'Angelo, LICSW, LMFT, Bruce Minor, LMFT, Briar Miller, LMFT, and Michelle Libi, LMFT.

You blink and end your repose to find that you're alone. It feels as if you have awoken from a dream. You rise from your resting spot and begin to walk down the winding path toward the sound of a river. As you walk, you notice the crunch of twigs underfoot and hear distant birds. Is one of them the red-winged blackbird? Neither your bird friend nor the forest yeti are anywhere in sight. Perhaps you dreamed them.

You look up at the branches of a nearby tree and notice a small silver shape clinging to a twig. Pausing, you raise up onto your tiptoes and realize that this is a cocoon, perhaps belonging to a butterfly or a moth. You gaze at the cocoon for a moment longer, noticing it shake as the small creature inside struggles with its transformation. *Change is such hard work,* you muse, and resume the hike. As you walk you notice that you have many aches in your body. How long were you sitting in meditation? You stretch your neck from side to side as you continue to make your way down the mountainside. As you breathe in, the air is fragrant with the scent of dried leaves and warm earth. You wonder at the way the seasons seem to have shifted around you on your travels. As you look around the forest bordering either side of the path, you notice hints of yellow and orange in many of the leaves. The wind shifts, blowing the undersides of the leaves up, causing them to shift and sway. It reminds you of a distant memory, but as you grasp for it, the memory skitters out of reach.

The path winds down the slope, and you lean slightly backward against the tug of inertia and gravity. The sun's rays are just the right amount of warm, offering a radiating blanket of heat against the cooler air temperature. You look down and slightly to your left, and you see a ribbon of blue snaking through the undergrowth far below: a river. It looks like a nice place to pause and rest. You estimate that you have at least another mile to walk down the mountain before you reach the riverbank. You walk down toward it.

Therapy's Big Brother

Once upon a time, as Bruce Minor reminds us, we were all just psychotherapists. In the very, very beginning of our industry, there were just small to medium-sized collectives of human beings throughout the American and European continents—composed mostly of wealthy men and a few audacious women—gathering together in an attempt to suss out the nature of the human mind and heart. From these meetings, the field of psychoanalysis was born. While these early theorists and practitioners engaged in practices that we would gasp at today—Freud psychoanalyzing his daughter,[2] Jung sleeping with several of his patients who then became therapists-in-training[3]—their mistakes became the foundations upon which rules like "no dual relationships" were based.

These early therapists did not have insurance agencies or managed care with which to deal. But they also tended to focus on treating the bourgeoisie—the European upper middle class who could afford to pay for things like this newfangled "talking cure," thanks to their monopoly on industry. Neither Jung, Adler, nor Freud himself (founding psychoanalysts all) had to consider whether high-quality psychotherapy happens in increments of forty-five, sixty, or ninety minutes. We bring you this abbreviated history lesson to remind us all that our present constructs have not always existed. Not only have they not always existed, but they might not actually be the most effective structure for treatment.

When family therapy was new, co-therapy and one-way mirrors with reflection teams were the standard of the day. When Justine tells graduate students about these once-standard training practices, they are in awe. "But how did that get paid for?!" they exclaim. The short answer is that decades ago, universities, particularly public universities, had more money in the humanities and social science departments. Insurance once reimbursed for far more therapeutic services than they do now. Then Justine will often go on to tell her students about sitting in her own graduate school classroom at Hazelden Graduate School of Addiction Studies (now Hazelden Betty Ford) and hearing her professors talk about the changing landscape of drug and alcohol treatment. In the beginning, they would say, anything could be covered as long as the client was admitted to an inpatient drug treatment facility; but once insurers discovered that too many folks (in their opinion) were getting drug and alcohol treatment, it suddenly became a three-ring circus's worth of hoops to jump through in order to get folks into residential drug and alcohol treatment.

Structured limitations are necessary for high-quality therapy (recall the example of sandtray therapy and the need for a literal box within which to put the sand, from chapter 2). Certainly, the case could be made that American psychoanalysis and drug treatment of the 1970s and 1980s was in need of a bit more clinical oversight. But the evolution that followed brings us to a dystopian present where third-party payers like insurance companies are dictating the terms and conditions of treatment. They're also dictating the amount of money that the clinician receives for the work they do based solely on their licensure, rather than on the type of work they're doing. These payouts are often inadequate at best and paltry at worst. Because of variable reimbursement rates, the amount of time and effort needed to handle billing issues, and the hoops clinicians need to navigate to get even the small amount of money they're paid, private-practice clinicians are increasingly opting out of the insurance model. This causes frustration for would-be clients, and for other clinicians.

Licensure Drama

Have you ever had an issue with another clinician and thought, "Well, that's just because they're a Ph.D.; doctorate school sucks all of the fun out of you"? Or perhaps you've thought, "They don't teach master's-level clinicians anything about diagnostics." Third-party payers and clinicians determine their reimbursement or compensation rates based on a number of factors, including education. Hierarchical thinking dictates that the more education and experience a person has, the more they should be valued. The main way that we express or show value is through monetary compensation. However, this very quickly leads to confusion and resentment when master's-level clinicians and doctoral-level clinicians are working at the same practice or agency and are performing, at least on paper, the same job functions. Disparate training and licensure requirements can lead to differences in case conceptualizations, standards of care, and clinical interventions.

Certainly these varied perspectives can be helpful if discussed and processed through open and honest clinical dialogue. But who has time for that? We don't say this to minimize or undermine the value of care coordination. The reality, though, is that third-party payers don't reimburse for care coordination. Contemporary clinicians are lucky if they can connect for five or ten minutes via phone either just before the beginning (seven a.m.) or just after the end (seven p.m.) of their clinical day. Thus, it's no surprise that confusion and even infighting across licenses and education levels abound.

Justine recalls a question from a student about this infighting: "But who is actually above the others? There has to be a hierarchy, right?" Justine responded that while it may feel as though there is a hierarchy, the reality is that we're a community with a variety of skills. We don't need to fight among ourselves. She said that just because someone with a doctorate has more education than someone with a master's degree, that doesn't make them better than or above the master's-level clinician. This is a social construct that we get to question and challenge, because it no longer serves us. The tangible difference between master's-level and doctoral-level clinicians lies in the area of assessment. Folks who complete doctoral programs are schooled in the practice of psychological assessment and usually graduate with the third-party-payer reimbursable skill of psychological assessment.

With gravity on your side, you make it to the bottom of the mountain faster than anticipated. The sound of the river rings in your ears as you push through the bracken toward the riverbank. The grass along the shore is a deep green and only slightly prickly as you kneel down and bend over the water, cupping your hands to take a long, cool drink. Once you have quenched your thirst, you sit back on your heels and stare out across the blue water, leaning into the rays of the sun at your back. You notice a butterfly flapping its wings and landing on a nearby flower.

App Therapy Is the New In-Home Therapy

Newly minted therapy graduates find themselves staring down the gauntlet of the licensure process, which usually entails several examinations, hours of supervision, and even more hours of direct client care. Depending upon the state where you live and the license you're pursuing, you may find it very difficult to get a job that pays you money while you acquire hours you can count toward licensure. Over the past few decades, the entry-level job for graduates in this predicament was in-home family therapy. Often considered the grunt work of the therapy industry, in-home family therapy requires practitioners to work long hours and drive long distances for very minimal pay. In 2014, when Larisa was working as an in-home clinician, she didn't even make minimum wage, so she worked another job part time as an after-hours crisis counselor.

Today's graduates have a new, additional option: they can become app therapists. Similar to other gig jobs like Uber Eats and Lyft, clinicians who work for therapy apps such as BetterHelp, TalkSpace, and Larkr are either associately licensed or fully licensed clinicians, and they work entirely through their company's telehealth app interface. They tend to have very large caseloads (pitched to them as a "great opportunity to get your licensure hours"), minimal time with an assigned supervisor, and demanding clinical expectations. Most therapy app jobs market their services to prospective clients with the promise of a readily available therapist, translating to the expectation that the therapist is available to the client at least via chat through most hours of the day and night.[4]

Larisa vividly recalls many of her lectures with Dr. Anne Ramage for a number of reasons, not the least of which is that Dr. Ramage is an excellent professor and an enigmatic speaker. Among all of Larisa's memories of Dr. Ramage's Carl Whitaker quotes and experiential role-plays, she recalls the professor advising time and again that "in-home jobs will be waiting for you as soon as you graduate. They're tough. You need to be ready. But they'll give you excellent experience in working with families." Then Dr. Ramage discussed the MFT techniques from that particular lecture that might apply to in-home work, and she explained the basic safety strategies of which in-home clinicians needed to be aware.

When Larisa graduated, she did indeed take a job as an in-home family therapist. The night before her first day, she reviewed the strategies she had learned from Dr. Ramage:

1. Arrive five minutes early, and look up the homes you'll be visiting in advance so you can plan your parking strategy. Never

schedule sessions late in the evening or after dark.
2. Be ready to set clear and consistent boundaries, and for those boundaries to be tested.
3. Pack a change of clothes and hand sanitizer.
4. Review your agency's privacy policies.
5. When you enter someone's home, assess for safety and your own exit strategy. Although it is rare that clients will ever mean you harm, things can and do get out of hand when you are in the family's own space. You get to protect yourself first.

This survival guide doesn't apply to folks who are working for therapy apps, but the need for both support and coping strategies is no less acute. If you're working for a therapy app, we, the authors, offer you deep compassion and the following tips:
1. Plan an exit strategy. What does this mean? It means a human being can't sustain years of work at the rate demanded by therapy apps. So it's essential for you to decide how long you can sustain working for a therapy app before you go the way of a younger Larisa and start losing your hair and developing insomnia.
2. Find a supervisor outside the therapy app. Yes, you will probably have to pay for this

supervision, and that will likely cause financial stress. However, it is crucial for you to have a guide whose sole investment is in you and who exists outside the system in which you work, to help you regain perspective and hold boundaries around things like time management and availability.

3. Remember that any symptoms of *burnout* (i.e., signs of physical or emotional distress) you're experiencing are likely the cause of *moral injury* —harm caused by the system in which you work—rather than any fault of your own (we'll discuss these concepts in more detail in the next section of this chapter).

4. Manage your expectations for yourself. However you envisioned your therapy experience, it likely did not involve a smartphone application called "Better-something." You can't do depth psychotherapy in this kind of context; what you can do is help your clients with basic coping strategies and compassionate presence—sometimes, but not all the time. You're not required to have 24/7 availability, no matter what your company tells you. Not even standard laptops can run constantly forever; they need to rest and update.

5. Reach out to your community. When you work in an online environment, it can be difficult to get your emotional needs met. Please remember to engage with other living beings outside your work environment who understand some of what you're going through and who can show up for you.

Burnout and Moral Injury

The Realm of Our Work has changed in ways that we never imagined over the course of the collective traumas of the 2020s. Suddenly the norm is to work in a virtual therapy room, and some clients expect to have regular access to their therapist via text messages and video chat services. This isn't what we thought the field would look like. When Justine imagined her future as a therapist, she saw herself engulfed in a scarf, with a teacup in hand, sitting across from her client in an overstuffed chair near a small fire in a fireplace, surrounded by books. She envisioned herself helping people and feeling filled up by the work, then returning home to a pleasant evening all to herself—overall a very calm and steady way of life.

This is not reality. For a time she did have the tea and the overstuffed chair, but the rest of the fantasy was just that—a fantasy. Justine now works behind a computer and sits in a rolling chair; her view is full of microphones, a ring light, and multiple monitors. For her, the change in our industry has been the death of a dream. The death of any dream is an ambiguous loss that even therapists are not always good at recognizing and finding compassion and ritual to help them move through it.

Of course, parts of what Justine imagined the life of a therapist to be all those many years ago, before she ever entered the field, were simply inaccurate. Even before teletherapy and therapy apps took over the field, the life of a therapist was rarely calm and steady. It had moments and longer periods of such calm, but the nature of therapy is to work with volatile emotions. The emotional intensity inherent to the profession impacts even the most experienced and boundaried of therapists.

Larisa's experience differed in that she had a logical view of what life in the field would be like. She felt like she had prepared herself emotionally for the trials of holding space for people and their emotions day in and day out. She believed that this preparation would act as a shield against any future catastrophe. The sadness came when she realized that no matter how prepared she had been, the situation was worse, and far more unpredictable, than she could have imagined. She was ready for the stresses of people's everyday lives and even for their great despair and trauma, but she was unprepared for the collective trauma of our age stepping into the therapy room and into her own life. She was totally unprepared for how political leadership would fail her and everyone else in her country during this time of great collective need. In her younger and more impressionable years, she believed that even though power is corrosive and toxic to politicians, when they were faced with clear and present disaster they would channel their highest selves and work to help people. Now Larisa realizes that America's representative government has devolved into rule by the wealthy elite who use their resources to buffer themselves from the pain and the needs of their constituents. Sometimes the despair she feels is crushing. Perhaps you can relate.

As we sit with the tragedies that have befallen our profession, it is no wonder that so many therapists struggle with burnout. Burnout can be defined from many perspectives. For the sake of brevity and clarity, we offer definitions of both individualized burnout and systemic burnout. Individualized burnout occurs when a person is so emotionally exhausted that they chronically struggle with depersonalization, which is emotional, physical, and cognitive numbness that makes the person unable to feel present in their own body or life.[5]

Systemic burnout is also known as *moral injury*, which is when a person experiences symptoms through no fault of their own; rather, the symptoms result from harm caused by the system in which they work. Moral injury was first defined by psychiatrist Jonathan Shay as a "betrayal of what is right by someone who holds legitimate authority in a high stakes situation."[6] Wendy Dean, Simon Talbot, and Austin Dean expanded upon this definition when they argued for clinician burnout to be redefined as moral injury:

> Moral injury occurs when we perpetrate, bear witness to, or fail to prevent an act that transgresses our deeply held moral beliefs. In the health care context, that deeply held moral belief is the oath each of us took when embarking on our paths as health care providers: Put the needs of patients first. That oath is the lynchpin [sic] of our working lives and our guiding principle when searching for the right course of action. But as clinicians, we are increasingly forced to consider the demands of other stakeholders—the electronic medical record (EMR), the insurers, the hospital, the health care system, even our own financial security—before the needs of our patients. Every time we are forced to make a decision that contravenes our patients' best interests, we feel a sting of moral injustice. Over time, these repetitive insults amass into moral injury.[7]

The article quoted above speaks solely to the experience of medical doctors, but its implications are clear for the chronic systemic burnout faced by so many in helping professions, including (but not limited to) therapists, medical technicians, nurses, and case managers. Helping professionals are increasingly placed in a double bind; that is, they're being placed in situations from which there is no escape, and they're being asked to perform at least two mutually exclusive actions simultaneously. They're being asked to care for clients but also to please many other stakeholders, all without the amount or quality of support that they need. Just like all double binds, this is an untenable situation that causes distress within the clinician.

We, the authors, appreciate the distinction between burnout and moral injury. The concept of moral injury takes the onus off the individual, because there's not enough self-care in the world to account for a system that's set up as a no-win situation. When larger systems talk about "burnout," that terminology allows them to let themselves off the hook for the clinician's pain. The system can then pass the problem back to the clinician as a personal failing, rather than a systemic one. The therapy field is currently crying out for systemic change. We cannot do everything and be everything to everyone. It is impossible, and it is destroying us.

The butterfly's orange and black wings flutter back and forth as it buries its face in a black-eyed Susan. You contemplate the effort that it took for this butterfly to metamorphose from a caterpillar. It went through a violent transformation in the cocoon to become this creature. It's not a pretty process. The butterfly must flap and flap and flap its wings inside the cocoon to strengthen them. It can be a difficult struggle to watch, and an onlooker often wants to help the butterfly be free from its enclosure. But if it's released from the cocoon early, the butterfly won't have the strength to fly and survive. It must struggle to become strong. As you stare at the butterfly, considering its beautiful wings, you start to breathe into your own bodily awareness. You notice the many places where you're holding tension and feeling stiff and sore. Perhaps you have also been flapping your metaphorical wings, becoming something new.

Grieving Tools—The Pain Paradox

As you might remember from chapter 2, pain can be a pivotal part of the meaning-making process. When paired with reflection time, pain can help us learn about our core values and live a life in accordance with them. Yet because we work in a field that values sacrifice and the pain that entails, therapists are also far more susceptible to what Freud would call the martyr complex, and what we refer to as hero/savior/sacrifice syndrome. The pain paradox explores the tension between pain as both catalyst for change and a state of prolonged suffering. Particularly in helping professions, suffering for our work is often framed as positive, meaningful, or altruistic. This harmful social construct can lead clinicians to stay in harmful jobs "for the sake of the clients" and sacrifice their own health in the process.

The pain paradox invites clinicians to question their social constructs around both pain and meaning-making. In the therapy room, the pain paradox is a tool that clinicians can use to help clients who are themselves engaging in harmful behaviors for the sake of "meaningful pain." Let us explore how you can use the tool of the pain paradox as you navigate your personal struggles outside of session, and how to use this tool with clients inside the therapy space.

Client

Pain is not the enemy, nor is it to be avoided at all costs. Sometimes what brings clients to therapy is the erroneous idea that we, their therapist, can help them learn how to disengage with their feelings entirely because these feelings are causing them pain. Of course, the reality is that we can teach them distress tolerance skills to be present with their pain and their feelings so they can learn to listen to the important messages carried by their feelings.

However, clients can sometimes mistake pain for purpose. We see this frequently with our creative clients. So often the idea of the "crazy artist" takes hold of clients. Several of Justine's clients were terrified of feeling better.

They believed that their sickness and the distress it caused fueled their art. But the reality was that after going through treatment, these clients were all able to continue making amazing art, and in fact they did so with more frequency and focus. Another part of the process of working with these folks is helping them see that they're full human beings who are more than just the art they craft. Many fear that if they lose the art then they lose themselves and they no longer matter. However, in our experience, part of their healing journey entails exploring areas of their life outside of art. Eventually, they come to see their art as but an aspect or a planet within the vast cosmos of their lives.

Therapist

For many of us, the desire to make meaning from our own pain drew us to the field of psychotherapy. Most therapists have experienced some type of mental distress, whether it's childhood trauma, an eating disorder, bullying, discrimination, or an abusive relationship with chemicals. For many of us, surviving this kind of pain was only the first phase of the healing process, with the second phase being meaning-making.

The pain paradox is a gentle invitation for therapists to carefully consider ways to cultivate meaning and joy outside the therapy field. Although our work as therapists is absolutely meaningful, it is also back-breakingly painful at times. If you don't have other avenues or ways to make meaning and find purpose, you'll find it even more challenging to take breaks from the field, regardless of how long such a break lasts, because you struggle to see the "you" outside the office. You need not try something life altering or huge. When Larisa was recovering from a severe case of moral injury, she began making playlists, an activity she had not engaged in since her college days. This small daily activity helped her to begin to reconnect with playful and creative energies outside her clinical and professional work.

The difficult message that Justine received was that her time as a direct-care therapist was coming to a close. After over a decade of work, and so many clients helped, she began to feel that her meaning-making was now to be found in the classroom, on the stage, and on the page. She experienced a great deal of pain as a therapist during the pandemic and the social justice uprising, but the pain invited her to consider where new meaning could from. The answer was that it was time to guide the next generation of clinicians and to hold the hands of those who are still in the trenches. As of this writing, Justine is currently working on the slow transition out of direct client care.

Due North: Self of the Therapist

One of the struggles inherent in walking the dialectic between the system and the individual is despair. In the case of moral injury, which is caused by a series of broken systems subjecting clinicians to harmful double binds, it can feel like there's little or nothing for a therapist to do beyond retiring from the field. While this certainly is an option, we offer you another one: harm reduction and intentional activism. As you may already know, the harm-reduction model of addiction recovery focuses on making small, actionable changes that mitigate abusing behaviors, rather than prescribing total sobriety. Our intention is to invite you as a clinician to assess the harm you're currently facing in your career and how it's affecting you. You can't immediately change the systems in which you practice therapy, but you can make a concerted effort to mitigate the negative impact that these systems have upon you.

Some ways that you might limit the harm you experience include limiting the number of hours you work or the types of clients or clinical presentations with which you work. Perhaps you currently work in a place with an unreliable schedule, and that causes you distress; is it possible to have a more structured schedule? If you're not being given time for breaks or lunch, is this a conversation you can have and a boundary you can set with your site supervisor? These can be small or large changes, but any change can go a long way to help mitigate the harm you're experiencing. As clinicians, we're trained to think of harm reduction solely from the perspective of our clients. But when our current systems are causing us harm as well, then we must consider our safety and energy levels, too. As we discussed in the previous chapter, we're not caring for our clients when we're modeling self-harming behaviors.

If you work with insurance, then you're likely all too familiar with the time and content constraints placed on the clinical hour. It's becoming increasingly common to only reimburse for the 90837, 53–60 minute therapy billing code if the clinician is providing a specialized service like EMDR or en vivo exposure therapy. Even in instances where a clinician accurately assesses for additional time, insurers that enforce these restrictions will likely not authorize you to bill the 90837 code no matter how much additional clinical documentation you provide. In a scenario in which you know your client needs the 7 extra minutes but is paneled with an insurance provider who will not reimburse for a full hour of therapy, you can reframe those extra 7 minutes as a gift you're giving to your client rather than ending promptly at the 52.5 minute mark or spending hours of additional time arguing with insurance, all for naught.

Is this an ideal solution? No. But perhaps it is a solution that honors your therapeutic ethics, the client's therapy needs, and your own time. In the harm-reduction approach, there are no perfect solutions. The goal is to mitigate harm, not to solve problems perfectly. Consider what would make this even a little bit better right now. With the energy you have left from harm reduction, you can then make discerning choices about where to advocate for systemic change. Do you want to call your local legislators, join your licensure's national advocacy committee, engage a colleague in a conversation around privilege and clinical biases, or add another pro bono/low-sliding-scale client to your caseload?

Another consideration is that some sessions require more emotional energy than others, but sessions are reimbursed based on units of time, not units of emotional intensity. When Justine was working with her client who was dying, each session felt much longer than sixty minutes. The amount of emotional energy required in those sixty minutes was simply greater than that required in a session with a client who was struggling with, for example, social anxiety. We do not intend to minimize the struggle of social anxiety in any way. Rather, our intent here is to try to convey something that in modern times we struggle to quantify and to express: time is not the only measure of value within a discrete event.

Justine's practice runs entirely on a cash basis, so she didn't have to worry about insurance reimbursement. Ultimately, however, she was not paid more for more emotionally intense work. Insurance is its own challenge in these more complex cases, as the clinician must find clinical language to express the work that was done in the therapy room. "Fanficcing the afterlife" is not likely to get reimbursed. You can imagine—because you've probably had a similar experience—sitting down at your computer after a long day of emotionally fraught therapy sessions and then struggling to find the clinically appropriate language to, in effect, prove that you did therapy worthy of insurance reimbursement.

It feels as though we're fighting not just for pay, but also for basic recognition and respect for the work we do. The world doesn't realize that we're performing the roles of multiple different types of healers, and we're expected to do so with grace and quiet. The image of the therapist as "giver" implies that we should want to give of our time and energy and shouldn't ask for anything in return, including a living wage. Unfortunately, within capitalism this is exploitative and unsustainable. We knew that the work would be hard, but many therapists find themselves surprised and saddened by the lack of structural support and the very real systemic reality that our current societal systems make it harder to do our work. Sometimes we're forced to choose between doing the intense work of meaningful therapy and conserving enough energy for ourselves so that we have something left at the end of the workday. This dilemma is not unique to the therapy profession; it plagues all the major helping professions, including doctors, veterinarians, nurses, teachers, medical aides, and home caregivers.

Due West: Supervision

Supervisees, if you find that you're already experiencing symptoms of burnout, take a moment to consider whether these symptoms might be more correctly described as an indication of moral injury. Is your employer putting you in a double bind? If so, bring this information to your supervisor and ask for support. If your supervisor is new to the concept of moral injury, feel free to show them this book, or link them to an article. If they won't engage with this line of inquiry, that is great information that might suggest you should seek additional or different supervision. You deserve to have a supervisor who wants to change the system to improve equity for your future career.

Supervisors, you're in a powerful position to move the field in a more equitable direction. Even if you're not a site supervisor, you get the opportunity to meet with preclinical therapists who seek you out for your guidance. These preclinical therapists work in a variety of contexts, and you get to hear about the moral injuries firsthand. We invite you to begin to tell your supervisees when you see that they're caught in a double bind, and offer them the harm-reduction strategies that you feel comfortable sharing. It's not uncommon for supervisees to believe that any burnout symptoms they're experiencing are due to their own naivete, and it's crucial for them to understand that while they do have a role in their own experience, they can only control so much.

This is a hard message, supervisors, but you must also pay attention to your own levels of burnout and moral injury. Supervisees depend on you to guide them through their metamorphosis, and if you find that you don't have the stamina to sit with them as they move through the process, then it's probably time for you to take a step back from providing direct supervision. And sometimes we don't realize that we're part of the morally injurious problem until we gain new information. For instance, Justine used to take on unpaid graduate-level interns, which she made sense of because she was giving them so much of her time. And while she indeed was offering them her sage wisdom, charging clients for their services without offering the interns any of that income made Justine part of the systemic problem that leads to moral injury.

Due East: Education

Students, please be advised that it's not your sole responsibility to avoid burnout, even when it's presented to you that way. You're often told that if you do everything "right" and "win" at self-care, then burnout will never happen to you. This is disingenuous. Burnout can happen to any of us, even when we have the best of intentions and a comprehensive self-care plan. And of course the standard conception of burnout assumes that you're solely responsible for your well-being, which we know is not true. You might experience moral injury instead. Yes, it's important to have a self-care plan, of course. Yet it is not foolproof, and it's important to recognize the signs of toxicity in your workplace, both in terms of interpersonal relationships with other employees and more structurally broken or toxic systems.

Sadly, the mental health world is not immune to the challenges that all systems face. In some ways we are worse at facing such challenges, because we think we're better. We believe we could never exploit workers, because we know how not to; but that's not the case. Many new therapists are exploited by being asked to work for free during internships, to work outside of the scope of their practice, or to work with minimal supervision with some of the toughest clients in the business. This is unreasonable, and yet it's the way it's been done for years. We invite you to fight back against it. Refuse to be a part of systems that wish to do you harm in the name of doing good works. If you are able to choose your practicum site, get curious with them about how their system functions and how interns are treated. Ask other interns for their true and honest opinions. This will always be hard work, but you don't need to be the proverbial coal miner who needs a canary. The systems are broken, and the only way they'll change is for folks to refuse to be a part of them. We know there's a power dynamic here with you at the bottom, so please find a teacher or supervisor who shares your worldview, and allow them to help you work through this process.

Teachers, please be this person for your students. Even if you're not a practicum advisor, you can have an incredible impact on the early working life of your students. They need to know the realities of what's out there. We don't just treat clients; we also have to work in a broken system that's largely stacked against us. Insurance companies don't respect the work we do, and we're not paid fairly. People get burned out and leave the field. These are not fun messages to give during your lecture on Virginia Satir, yet they're true. The world she once practiced in has changed dramatically. Insurance companies won't pay for you to do a co-therapy experiential family diorama. Allowing students to believe that they'll be able to do the work they dream of in any scenario is a bait and switch. Yes, they can do this work in certain circumstances. The theories are important, and we love them; our forebears and their messages are our legacy. Also, the world is not set up to practice in the way that we teach students it is. There is a balance to walk between theory and practice, and this is an opportunity to set students up for success by helping them be aware of these dangers on the front end.

If you're a teacher and you're feeling burned out, of course you are. If you've been working with students who are collectively traumatized, that takes a lot of effort. Justine loves teaching, but it's hard work to present these realities to wide-eyed students who just want to do some good after so much awful has happened in the world. Many teachers go back to what they know best: clinical work. It's hard to be a truth-teller, and it's especially hard for those who want to continue to teach in the old ways, as students are becoming more aware of the real world and want to know how what they learn in school applies to folks who have different bodies, socioeconomic statuses, and political views. Not all teachers are prepared to have these conversations. If you're experiencing burnout for any of these reasons or others not mentioned here, please know that you're not alone. Many teachers feel this way. You are allowed to step away from education and return to clinical practice, or go on to something else, or get additional training so you can feel more prepared. This life is full of choices, and even if you thought teaching would spark joy, if it doesn't that's okay.

Due South: Death and Love

You pause by the river's edge and decide to stretch. You reach high up to the sky, remembering the towering yeti that you met, and you wonder where she is now. You notice the thought and allow it to drift away, like the leaves you see drifting downstream. You open your arms wide like the red-winged blackbird, and you remember its call and all it did to help you on your journey. You reach low toward your toes and remember the merperson diving deep into the cool, still pond and the lessons they taught you about the duality of nature. You rock gently from side to side, remembering the playful honey badger who refused to conform. You rise back up and place your hands on your heart, soaking in the feeling of gratitude for all you have learned, soaking up this place in this moment.

You listen to the rushing river and begin to join your breath to the rhythmic sound, and then you lie down by the water's edge. You reach into your pack and take out your journal, placing it on your chest. You lie here for a long time, sometimes thinking and sometimes drafting the contours of the region into your journal, always returning to your breath. After a while you decide it's time to move again, but first you pause and consider that you can decide in any moment that this is the death of that moment, of that practice, and that you are reborn into the world. In this moment as you prepare to get up from your rest, it's the death of your meditation practice. Death does not need to be full of sorrow. There are moments in life when we can choose to end and decide what we'll leave on the grass when we depart and what we'll take with us. What will you leave and what will you take with you in this moment of death?

In this penultimate realm of our grief, you've been faced with the wreckage of our field. So much about the way we practice has changed, and so much of what we love about the work of therapy is lost. As we sit together in these ruins, we invite you to consider which aspects of the work you might want to lay to rest—to, in essence, return to the earth. Perhaps teletherapy has been a gift to you and your family, opening up windows of time and possibility that you didn't have when you were consumed with a commute. In this case, you might say goodbye to in-person therapy and put that metaphorical stuffed chair to rest. The rebirth of your clinical practice lies in virtual healing. Perhaps your expectations of control and autonomy are dying. You can let go of the expectation to be the best, calmest clinician and instead begin the process of becoming an authentic and present therapist—present to both the calm and the turmoil. There can be relief in letting go. You did what you could. Now it's time to rise and decide what you'll do next.

10

THE REALM OF OUR MEANING

*I'll see you all
this coming fall
in the big rock candy mountains*

—HARRY MCCLINTOCK

We now reach our final realm. Every realm you've journeyed through has invited you to question the nature of your reality. Here in this final chapter, you can commence crafting the reality in which you want to live. While this can feel like an overwhelming task, it's also quite freeing. There are no wrong answers here; there is only your imagination and the invitation to imagine what could be—to imagine Utopia.

It might seem strange to think about Utopia in a book centered around grieving the ravages of our past and facing the horrors of our present cultural moment. We invite Utopia in now for several reasons, not the least of which is that late-stage capitalist society often misunderstands the concept of Utopia. Life in Utopia is not an easy or pain-free existence. Utopia can only exist when we as a species are ready to sit down with our pain and work together to create systems and ways of being that increase our ability to be present. But what would these systems even look like?

To help us chart a course in this bold new realm of meaning-making, we will be inviting in many sages. First, Dutch historian and Utopian advocate Rutger Bregman has a few insights and a few mistakes to offer. Early in his career, Rutger was a great believer in the power of reason to create a Utopia of the future. He extolled the virtues of past civilizations that strove for a higher ideal—or, dare we say, "a more perfect union"—and was generally quite critical of Indigenous cultures and precivilization societies.[1] Like so many before him, he fell victim to the social construct of progress, which is the belief that modern society is an improvement on all cultures and societies that came before it. Put simply, Rutger's first published conception of Utopia was a Dystopia (and in the history of Utopian thought, this is actually quite common). He learned from these missteps, and in his most recent work, *Humankind: A Hopeful History*, Rutger explores the history of kindness and compassion fostered by so many of the precivilization nomadic peoples. He also lauds the virtues of contemporary Indigenous folks.[2] We invoke Rutger to step forward as our first sage in this chapter because of how he failed. Utopia is a process, not a destination.

Feeling refreshed and rejuvenated after some mindful stretches underneath the warm sun, you stand and survey your surroundings. The river is wide but not too wild, and as you scan along to both the north and the south you don't see any rapids or problematic rocks. You lift both hands to shield your eyes—the shore on the other side looks to be at least a mile or so away; too far for you to swim (you are not of the merfolk, after all), but decidedly doable if you were in a boat.

The wind kicks up and you blink your eyes. As you push the hair out of your face, a flash of light catches the corner of your eye. You turn and notice what appears to be a small canoe lying on its side. You walk over and gently roll the canoe back up, searching to see if there happen to be any oars nearby. In the belly of the two-person craft, you spot one oar and reach toward it only to find that it has been broken in half. Ain't that just the way? But perhaps its match is lying about somewhere. You widen your search to explore the brush farther up the bank; after several minutes, you come to the conclusion that the broken oar is all you have to work with. You return to the canoe and inspect the broken oar. It might be workable if you hunch. Returning both pieces of the oar to the belly of the canoe, you move to the back and begin to push it out toward the water, doing your best to time it just right so you don't get wet feet.

You don't succeed in dry feet, but you get yourself and the canoe into the water, and you begin to move with the current. Trying to paddle across the river with your nub of an oar is difficult. You paddle a few strokes on one side of the canoe, then a few strokes on the other, trying to keep yourself going straight. It's tiring, and your back is starting to hurt. But as you get about a quarter of the way across, you see another boat coming toward you—it is two of your old friends from the campfire whom you met so many miles ago at the start of this grieving journey! They wave, and you give yourself permission to stop paddling for a moment and let them catch you. You greet one another and discuss your travels a bit. These adventurers tell you there is a group of friends on the other side of the river. They see you struggling on your own with your little nub of an oar, and they offer you one of their paddles in exchange. The two canoers can switch off using the proper oar and the nub. You thank them, and they offer you well wishes on the rest of your journey. You continue on toward the shore, filled with gratitude for the friends you've met and the gifts they've offered. Your journey would be impossible alone.

Imagination Station

We've been through a lot, whether we're seasoned practitioners, new therapists, or students just starting out. The road was uncharted, and you picked up the gauntlet and began to chart a course for yourself and for all those who will come after you. Now that we all finally have a moment to breathe, in a canoe or wherever you might be, it's time for us to imagine what we want the future of our work and our lives to look like. We, the authors, invite you to practice something that is very important to us: imagination. Play therapists, narrative therapists, and experiential therapists all value the importance of the imagination, which allows us to consider what could be—what is possible. How will we rewrite the future of our field? Together.

Loss is a process that cracks us open. It changes us forever, and the only way to truly heal through loss is to change. Often this change involves creating new meaning in your life. Grieving entails change because in order to keep loving what you've lost, you must create a new way to exist with it. Throughout this book, we have invited you to reckon with the destruction and loss of our health, our climate, our politics, our faith, and our very way of life. But when something dies, something else is born in its place. And for those systems that continue on, if they're not how we want them to be, then we can decide that it's time for them to move on.

Now we come together and begin to imagine new and better systems—new and different ways of being. We can begin to consider other ways of working and living together that don't perpetuate the cycle of exploitation and violence. Utopia doesn't mean a world without pain; it just means having systems that support you while you experience pain. But since the process of Utopia can easily feel cumbersome and overwhelming, let's start with that necessary first step of imagination. Reality can very quickly get in the way of expansive thought because it keeps us bound to the negative constructs that continue to thrive in our contemporary American landscape. Let us look to the Afrofuturists. These philosophers, artists, and writers begin their work from a single point of imagination: What if the peoples of African cultural heritage played an equal and equitable role in the formation of the contemporary world? What if European colonizers had not marched their armies of destruction across the globe, enslaving the inhabitants of the lands they invaded and setting in motion the modern world, in which colonizer countries continue to monopolize resources and mainstream narratives?[3] This is a powerful reimagining of the world. The writing and theorizing taking place in these Afrofuturist spaces is the literal process of Utopia in action.

Let us embody this process for our field. Imagine for a moment what our field would look like if a therapist only had twenty clients in their lifetime (stay with us). For many of us, we are conditioned to think of meaning in terms of numbers. Thus, if I work with five hundred clients over the course of my career, surely that's more meaningful and important than just working with fifty. While so many fields have been despecialized for the sake of moving faster, therapy is one of a shrinking number of fields that have thus far avoided this pressure of industrialization. But we still bear the scars of productivity culture; many of us still think of our work and our impact in terms of quantifiable numbers. We invite you to imagine a system in which more is valued than numbers. Remember that we still don't have a way to fully measure and quantify emotions and emotional experiences like love, pain, and compassion. Yet our very profession is based on the primacy of emotions and emotional states.

When Justine was early in her preclinical process, she struggled with the idea of being a therapist. She was already a yoga teacher and an antiauthoritarian punk. She wondered why she couldn't just become a yoga therapist or a life coach, instead of jumping through all the hoops and paying all the fees to become a licensed therapist. Justine was fortunate to have a great supervisor who sat with her every week and had basically the same conversation each week. Justine would say, "Why am I doing this?" Her supervisor would sit and listen in compassionate silence as Justine lamented, and then the supervisor would ask Justine, "Why are you doing this?" To which Justine would respond that it felt important.

Justine had one other big concern: she worried that as a therapist she could only help so many people. During one particular supervision, Justine shared that as a yoga teacher, she could have a dozen people in a class; but as a therapist, she could only reach one person or family at a time. It didn't seem like enough. She believed her impact on the world wouldn't be felt. In response, her supervisor invited her to imagine a pond: "When you toss a rock into a still pond, it makes ripples that travel ever outward. So touching one life in fact means that we're reaching an uncounted number of other lives that we'll never know about. The rock that is one client influences that client's primary relationships in both family of origin and kin of choice, as well as their coworkers and the person they get their groceries from. Impacting one life has ripples. And the truth is that impacting even one life is enough. You are enough." Justine wasn't ready to see that as a young and wide-eyed therapist, but she sees it now. Now she has had the honor to pass this information on to her supervisees and students when they feel as though they or their work are not enough.

If we existed in a system that valued emotions and recognized the shifting emotional energies that many folks colloquially call "vibes," then we'd be able to integrate the importance of moving slowly. Relational and systemic change takes time. Not everything can or should be done quickly. We invite you to return to our original daydream. If you're a therapist who practices long-term therapy, then you already know it's important to learn the nuances of your clients' emotional states and the details of their lives. If you had twenty clients for your entire career, this might mean working with those twenty clients throughout their adult life span with varying degrees of treatment frequency based on therapeutic need rather than what insurance will reimburse for on a weekly or monthly basis.

You continue to row your boat. It takes longer than expected, even with the borrowed oar, but eventually you're just a few canoe lengths away from the riverbank. You lean forward and dig your oar into the water, pulling back so hard on it that your triceps burn. You look up to smiling faces as three of your friends splash into the water, grabbing the prow of your canoe and pulling you the rest of the way onto shore. You toss your paddle onto the grass, bracing your arms on both sides of your canoe as you hop out. One friend wraps you in a hug as the other shouts toward the clearing farther up the bank that they need to make room around the fire. You take off your pack and walk several yards toward the new yet familiar campfire. You gratefully accept a mug of fresh water and sit down among your friends. As you lean back against a tree, gently scratching your back against its serrated bark, you catch up with your friends and reflect on your respective journeys. You compare notes and maps of your travels. You mourn for those who aren't yet there and hope they make it.

Utopian Crafting

What led you to become a therapist? Perhaps it was the desire to make meaning from your past pain. Perhaps it was the desire to make up for what you perceived to be past mistakes. Perhaps you sought greater understanding about yourself and your fellow humans, and you equated understanding with meaning. Many folks turn to the healing professions to understand the human condition and to understand their own families and lives. Certainly, understanding is a kind of meaning. If you find that this meaning is all you need right now, then we invite you to stay here. We invite you to rest and to reflect and to acknowledge—perhaps even celebrate—all of this hard-won wisdom.

If you feel that having understanding is but the first step in the process of crafting Utopia, then join us here. It's one thing to understand an aspect of your life, such as your parents having not shown up as their best selves. But it's another thing to get curious about what that means to you and how it has profoundly shaped your life—and how it continues to, so that you now embody this change in your life. This place of curiosity can lead to a process of Utopia whereby you make meaning from this now felt and understood pain. Consider, if you will, the butterfly. It's one thing for the caterpillar to *understand* that it must go into a cocoon and dissolve into a sludge in order to become a butterfly. It's quite another to have the embodied experience of becoming a goo, and then growing a new body. A profound meaning is made through the embodiment, to fly with those hard-won wings to enjoy delicious floral elixirs with the other newly transformed butterflies.

As night falls, you and your fellow travelers prepare dinner and pour mugs of orange cream soda. You toast to one another and celebrate both your individual and communal quests! As the full moon rises, a fine mist begins to fall over the campsite, and one of your fellows throws another log on the fire. You close your eyes and breathe in the scents of pine, smoke, and cool night air. Your friend with hammered hoop earrings gasps beside you: "What is that?!" You open your eyes to see fourteen specters gliding toward you and your friends. They encircle the fire pit in a wide ring as you and your community huddle close to one another.

Two figures step forward, one in a vest and the other in shorts, holding hands and trading smiles. "We are the sages of the Realm of Our Plague. For us, Utopia was our collaborative friendship. Working together on books and discussing ideas was our highest expression of connection and community. We offer this: the story you are writing can always be revised. Utopia is never done."

You and your friends thank them for their gift.

A tall, imposing figure steps forward. Crossing her arms and grinning widely, she says: "I am the sage of the Realm of Our Health, and I am a black lesbian warrior poet. I am a mother. If I had succumbed to the rhetoric of my time, I would have died. But instead I forged a life of community and purpose. No one offered me Utopia—I made it. I wrote it. I offer you nothing. Your work is your own."

You and your friends bow your heads and contemplate her words.

Two figures step forward in turtlenecks and tweed. "We are the sages of the Realm of Our Earth. To remember us, one need only look up to the heavens or to the earth below, for we are all connected. We owe so much to one another and to the pale blue dot on which we stand. We offer you awe. May you find wonder in the majesty of each moment and treat each life you encounter with intention."

You and your friends take a moment to look up at the stars and the almost too-bright moon with wonderment and gratitude.

A figure carrying a badger steps forward. "We are the sages of the Realm of Our Origins. We are old friends and sparring partners. But here in this place beyond time, we are messengers. We bring you the gift of spontaneity.

May you never forget that life is a bizarre event, and the best way to engage in its strangeness is to meet it with your own."

You and your friends laugh. Truly, it is a wild thing to be alive.

A figure with a wise countenance steps forward. He makes eye contact with each member of the campfire before explaining, in a heavy Bronx accent: "I am the sage of the Realm of Our Kin. Each of you is a wonderful and unique being. You have something to offer your clients that only you can offer. But you must have the courage to really learn and be present with all parts of you. You must have the patience to really get to know and be present with your internal and external communities. Then and only then will you and your clients be able to transform. I believe in you, and I am so proud to walk among you."

You and your friends return his smile. As you feel his belief in each of you surround your community, you start to notice parts of yourself that you hadn't noticed before. Perhaps anything is possible—including loving yourself fully.

Two stalwart figures join this eclectic circle. One clears her throat while the other looks severely at you and your compatriots. "We are the sages of the Realm of Our Republic. Perhaps the least Utopian of systems, and the most in need of change. Death is all around you. Every moment matters. Do not shrink from uncomfortable truths. Face them. It is through honest confrontation that you will know true meaning."

You and your friends nod and swallow hard.

Two charismatic figures glide and sway into the circle. With smiles and nods to each camper, they intone: "We are the sages of the Realm of Our Faith. Do not be cowed by religious doctrine. The light of spirituality and faith sparks in us all. There is no meaning without our Gods and Goddesses—they are as varied as the stars. Creativity, imagination, and presence are the tools of Utopia."

You and your friends thank these sages and pull out your journals and maps to show them all you have discovered. They smile and nod.

One human draped in a scarf steps forward. "I am the sage of the Realm of Our Crisis. You have faced many struggles, and look; you moved through them with the power of your connection to each other, the earth, and your Selves. I leave you the gift of memento mori, the reminder of death. Remember each day that you will, in the future, fall away. This life will end. And that is a gift, because it keeps you present and grateful for the world you have."

You all breathe a sigh of gratitude and gently raise your hands to this sage.

A moment of quiet settles over the camp as each person lowers their gaze and reflects on their personal sages, mentors, and supervisors. You exhale these memories—whatever meaning you've made from these experiences need not weigh you down.

The last sage steps forward, looking a bit embarrassed to be joining such a prolific circle. He steadies his glasses and says: "I am the sage of this realm, and I offer you this: May you be humble. May you be kind. May you always be willing to start again. I offer my gratitude. I am honored to be included."

You and your friends move to stand, joining the ring of sages. You are one unbroken circle now.

Grieving Tools—Fanficcing the Future

The final grieving tool we will explore centers around "fanficcing"—that is, writing fanfiction about—the future. More specifically, this tool focuses on ways that clinicians and clients can begin to explore the concept of Utopia. This is why we invite you to start imagining Utopia both inside and outside of session. It gives you the opportunity to learn about a side of yourself unfettered by oppressive working conditions, and it creates a space to practice envisioning different ways of being.

Now more than ever, it's clear that many of our current social structures and systems don't serve us. But to create new and sustaining systems, we must first give ourselves permission to imagine other realities—even other Utopias—that foster both individual and collective growth and healing. If we don't begin to cultivate this practice both within ourselves and during our clinical session, we doom ourselves to an untimely death.

Client

Consider how you already use the Utopia tool with your clients. You might use different language for this, perhaps calling it "the miracle question" from solution-focused therapy. But it differs in that we acknowledge that not everything can be as it should be. Just like in a garden, we can't have both bunnies and hawks, both flowers and weeds, without them impacting each other. Better to consider the story that the client wishes to live inside: the story of being a part of a torturous system, or the story of being a revolutionary on the field of battle for social change. Or anywhere in between. This doesn't need to be a binary, either all in or all out. It's okay to enter the battle at certain times and to retreat at others, or to spend time at the edge of the battlefield, and sometimes to go to the tavern in town and chat with the villagers.

Therapist

Therapists, in what story do you want to live? Do you want to be part of an oppressive system? Do you want to fight against it? Do you want to be somewhere else entirely?

We're living in a time of profound upheaval and change. The dual sides of change are death and birth. For human beings, the imagination is the birthplace of systemic change. We invite you to actively think about and talk about the kind of Utopia you would like to enact. Perhaps your Utopia incorporates daily naps for all citizens. Perhaps your Utopia reimagines the higher education system as a place of communal learning where anyone who wants to learn about Kant can study his life and works. Such a Utopia disassembles the ivory towers and rebuilds them as integral parts of the community. Your Utopia might involve monthly festivals where everyone takes turns cooking for each other. The key is to give yourself permission to imagine a future that values kindness and makes space for both pain and joy.

Due North: Self of the Therapist

What is your Utopia? Remember that Utopia is not about perfection but rather how to best support one another and ourselves through the pains and joys of life. How much of this Utopia are you enacting in your life and work right now? Just notice what comes up for you without assigning any judgment to what you find. For some, the idea of Utopia might feel too grand or imposing a topic to consider. If so, you might find it easier to try an alternate framing device: retirement. In America, people talk about retirement the way medieval Europeans fantasized about Cockaigne, an imaginary place of extreme luxury and ease. In retirement, you're no longer servant or slave to the clock. Retirement can be an existence where your time is restored to you and you get to decide how best to exist. Yet even those financially privileged few Americans who attain literal retirement struggle with this open-ended existence. An existence without limit or restriction can be overwhelming, boring, or terrifying by turn.

Pick whichever phrasing resonates with you, be it "Utopia," "retirement," or "time to myself," and begin to consider what meaningful ease would look like for you. For Larisa—whose propensity to overbook, overschedule, and overwork herself was the only existence she knew for her first thirty years of life—this concept of retirement felt initially daunting. She vividly remembers saying to a supervisor during her final year as a provisionally licensed clinician: "If I'm not working, then who am I?" Her supervisor gave her a stern stare and said, "That is something you need to figure out, or you'll never know yourself."

Never one to back out of a dare, it took Larisa five years and many losses before she was finally able to answer the question of who she was outside of work—and, perhaps just as important, what mattered to her outside of completed projects and checked-off to-do lists. In recent years, Larisa has found both meaning and power in lingering, daydreaming, and open-ended weekends where she moves with the flow of events rather than attempting to force plans into being. While kindness and compassion have always been cornerstones of her work as a therapist, Larisa finds meaning and joy in bringing these values into her daily life outside her work as a therapist, writer, and researcher.

Cultivating presence in each moment has helped her see the benefits of a life beyond the thrum and deluge of productivity. As an elder millennial, Larisa has no illusions about reaching retirement; she knows it's an unlikely destination for her and so many. Rather than waiting for systemic Utopia, she tries to thread experiences of joy, presence, and having enough into her daily life. In her clinical work, she invites clients to sit with the idea of what enough support would look like. They often observe together that Utopia is not about having the most, or having more than other living beings. It's about having access to enough of what really makes you joyful, and sharing this access with others.

Due West: Supervision

Supervisees, you deserve a supervisor who is ready and able to join you in facing the challenges and emotional turmoil caused by an ailing planet and a collapsing infrastructure. Facing the suffering of so many as social systems continue to fail us is overwhelming. You deserve a supervisor who will sit with you in times of sadness and despair while also holding hope.

When Justine was a supervisee, she brought a concern to her supervisor: someone had copied the wording from her website verbatim and used it as their own. She was understandably upset, but she definitely was not leading from her highest Self in confronting the person who had taken her intellectual property. Justine's supervisor invited her to see this person's humanity, not to excuse their behavior but to view it through a lens of compassionate understanding: "It's a good website. This person wants their website to be successful, too." It took some convincing, but Justine came to see the humanity in this other person. Years later, Justine co-created Therapeutic Fanfiction predicated on the idea that stories and ideas cannot and should not be owned in the conventional capitalist sense. This painful experience became a part of a series of catalyzing events that helped Justine question received social constructs and start to think creatively about the kind of world she wanted to intentionally create.

As we face the often terrifying reality of the dissolution of societal structures we once took for granted, like a functioning representative democracy and sustainable supply chains, supervisors have the opportunity to bring conversations of Utopia into the supervision space. Put another way, the death of old systems brings with it space for new ideas and ways of being to grow. Holding space for grief in supervision also means cultivating hope, community, and Utopia. As you invite your supervisees to be present with their feelings of sadness and loss, you can ask them to consider the parts of the old systems they miss, as well as the parts that were never working well and that they might want to change. This is an opportunity to invite your supervisees to imagine the working world in which they wish to live. As the future of the field, they are in the best possible position to begin to demand change that previous generations of therapists have tolerated or perpetuated.

For example, Larisa once had a supervisee with a client whose insurance provider kept incorrectly denying them services. The client, a person in a marginalized ethnic group, shared with the supervisee that they were used to this kind of treatment, and that although they valued their therapy with the supervisee, they would have to end services. While neither Larisa nor her supervisee could change the private insurance system, they did work with the practice's billing department to verify that this client had coverage for therapy and was being denied in error. Then, Larisa, the supervisee, and the billing coordinator created a plan that involved the coordinator calling the client's insurance each week after their session to ensure that the session would be correctly processed and thus covered by insurance. Larisa invited the supervisee to be transparent with her client about this process: "The larger system of private insurance is failing your client. But we are building a smaller system that is effectively supporting your client in the way that they both need and deserve to be supported."

Due East: Education

Well, students, you've been on a heck of a journey. We recognize that some of what you've read might have you questioning your decision to be a part of this field. And we're not sorry for that. We want you to be sure. We want you to be aware. And we want you to have your Self in charge of your decision-making. We would never discourage anyone from joining the field; we also believe that a cloudy picture is painted for students about what they'll encounter out there. It's rarely the clients who are a problem. It's usually the systems and ourselves that are holding on to problems. So, students, if you haven't done this already, ask yourself why you're coming into this field and what you hope you accomplish. Also, you truly are the future of the field. If you join forces and act as one, you can change the face of it, but it will take concerted action as a community, not just one lonely intern tilting at windmills. Find each other and rally together to create the change you want to see in this world. We believe in you!

Teachers, ask students to reflect on the realities of the field, and please be honest about the state of things. It's hard to watch their eager faces turn from joy to pain, and yet it's kinder to let them know what's out there than to send them into the woods unprepared. Justine's students often ask why she "dwells" on the negative. To that she says, "I'm just presenting what's going on. It's neither positive nor negative. But your reaction is interesting..." So teachers, get curious and lean into the discomfort. We know it's hard, and it's not exactly what you were asked to do; and yet, isn't it? Part of training future therapists is honesty about what their lives will be like—the good, the bad, and the crispy.

Due South: Death and Love

As you look around the campfire into the faces of friends, colleagues, and compatriots, you realize just how long it has been since you were all together. Opportunities for restorative community are rare and meaningful. A philosopher might point out that the rarity or time-limited nature of these interactions is part of what makes them so meaningful. We don't have forever with those we love, and this limit helps us be more present with the time we have.

Utopia is neither infinite time nor infinite pleasure. Rather, we offer to you that Utopia is a series of systems that help us to regularly cocreate meaningful community and presence. Even around this campfire, there is the reminder of absence and even death. Life cannot be divorced from pain without losing its meaning. Consider the moments when you love or have loved your work as a therapist. What systems or structures help or helped to foster these moments? You might want to reflect on this question by either journaling or pondering. Some of the moments that have been most meaningful to us, your authors, are when we were able to inspire hope in our clients, and especially when we were able to find hope ourselves.

In IFS one of the names given to the therapist is "hope merchant." In times of great strife it can feel as though there's no hope to peddle, and that's when we must fill our own basket before we can take it out into the village to share with others. How is your supply of hope? Just notice, without assigning any judgment to what you find. We have certainly had our own moments, days, or even weeks when the hope coffers were low. The way we found to fill them is through engaging with one another and remembering the value that's inherent in our humanity, not just as therapists, but as humans. Kindness and compassion can see us through the darkest moments.

Take a few more moments and look around the campfire. These are moments of hope to keep inside your memory and to celebrate in the here and now. We are all here together, and we are committed to helping one another face the challenges of life from a place of *metta*, a place of lovingkindness.

GRIEVING SUPPORTS

While you can find many useful books, journal articles, and other scholarly pursuits in the endnotes, we offer here some works of art that have been particularly meaningful for us when we're struggling to tap into feelings of grief and loss. We offer these suggestions for times when you're looking for a starting place where you can begin to engage with your own grieving. You can create the safe container of knowing you'll experience a deep emotion for just one song, just one episode, just one book, and so on. In each category of grieving supports, we name our own go-tos for engaging big feelings, and we invite you to consider what yours would be. Not all of our suggestions are sad on their faces; rather, they tap into something within us. They're evocative, and they spark emotion.

We both listed items in each category, and you'll notice that our lists are not symmetrical in number or style. When we sat down with our internal systems, some parts wanted to add more in certain categories and fewer in others. Let this be a reminder to you that there is no correct number of grieving supports. We invite you to sit with your own Internal Family System and notice what is there without judgment.

MUSIC

- Larisa: "Into the West" by Howard Shore, vocals by Annie Lennox; "Glitter (Claudio Doza Remix)" by Patrick Droney
- Justine: "Hallelujah" by Jeff Buckley, written by Leonard Cohen; "Wash Away" by Joe Purdy; "Box of Rain" by the Grateful Dead, written by Phil Lesh and Robert Hunter; "Wild Horses" by the Rolling Stones, written by Mick Jagger and Keith Richards; "Jisas Yu Holem Hand Blong Mi," by the Melanesian Choirs

VISUAL ART

- Larisa: *La maison du Rueil* (The house at Rueil, 1882) by Édouard Manet; *Bordighera* (1884) by Claude Monet
- Justine: All works by Edward Gorey (1925–2000); *Super Emo Friends* series by JSalvador Ramos; depictions of robots/droids having a hard time

TELEVISION

- Larisa: "All Good Things...," *Star Trek: The Next Generation*, season 7, episodes 25–26, aired May 23, 1994

- Justine: "Carry On," *Supernatural,* season 15, episode 20, aired November 19, 2020; "Death's Door," *Supernatural,* season 7, episode 10, aired December 2, 2011; "Through the Looking Glass," *Lost,* season 3, episodes 22–23, aired May 25, 2007

FILM

- Larisa: *Gladiator* (2000), directed by Ridley Scott, written by David Franzoni, John Logan, and William Nicholson; *The Green Knight* (2021), directed, written, edited, and produced by David Lowery
- Justine: *The Lord of the Rings: The Return of the King* (2003), directed by Peter Jackson, written by Fran Walsh, Philippa Boyens, and Peter Jackson; *The Crow* (1994), directed by Alex Proyas, written by James O'Barr, David J. Schow, and John Shirley; *The Secret of NIMH* (1982), directed by Don Bluth, written by Don Bluth, John Pomeroy, Gary Goldman, and Will Finn

BOOKS

- Larisa: *Momo* (1986) by Michael Ende, translated by J. Maxwell Brownjohn; *Cloud Atlas* (2004) by David Mitchell

- Justine: *Maus* (1986) by Art Spiegelman; *Griffin & Sabine: An Extraordinary Correspondence* (1991) by Nick Bantock; *The Velveteen Rabbit* (1922, 1991) by Margery Williams

GAMING OR CRAFTING EXPERIENCES

- Larisa: *To the Moon* (2011), developed and published by Freebird Games; *Outer Wilds* (2019), developed by Mobius Digital, published by Annapurna Interactive
- Justine: Designing and tying mala necklaces; clipping, designing, and pasting magazine collages

An Experiential Gift for Others

We have spoken at length in this book about ways to show up for ourselves, our clients, and the people we love. Here we offer you a literal gift you can give them—Greeting Grief grieving cards (as opposed to greeting cards), for writing to those who have passed on: https://www.greeting-grief.com. While letter-writing to the deceased is an often-used therapeutic intervention, these cards allow you to invite another person to have a grieving experience, which they can choose to accept or decline. Justine feels a personal attachment to these gifts, as they were created by her sister-in-law in memory of Justine's father-in-law. This is a reminder that gifts can arise from our pain.

ACKNOWLEDGMENTS

We have so many beings to thank without whom this book would not be possible. We thank them in the manner of our book, through realms. In the Realm of Our Publishing, we must first and foremost thank our editor, Shayna Keyles. Shayna is the stalwart Gandalf to our sometimes wayward fellowship, whom we most desperately needed in order to carry this emotionally heavy burden to its rest. We are also most grateful to the entire team at North Atlantic Books and Penguin Random House. You believed that a couple of pop culture nerds could write a serious book and do it well.

Thank you also to our generous beta readers who helped to shine light into corners that we didn't even realize were dark: Nicole Cardarella-Gasper, LPCC, Calvin Hauer, LMFT, Ashley Myhre, LMFT, Paige Reitz, LCSW, and Brittani Oliver Sillas-Navarro, AMFT. In the Realm of Our Industry, so many wise people have helped us to become the clinicians, writers, and humans that we are. We cannot possibly name all of those who shaped us, so here are three sages who directly influenced our work on this book: Ginny D'Angelo, LICSW, LMFT, Patty Hlava, PhD, and Anne Ramage, PhD.

Finally, to the Realm of Our Kin. Thank you to our personal therapists, R and K, who sat with us as we sat with this book, and much gratitude to our "therapist" of the mindful movement variety, Tyler Stevens, CPT, BCS, who managed to brighten even our darkest days. We are indebted to our friend Rachel J. Wilkinson for guiding us through the world of tarot. Thank you to our long-suffering partners, Brian Edward Therens and Eli Mastin, who endured many months of weepy housemates and lived to tell the tale. And thank you to our beloved fur friends: Hela, Thor, Merlin, Katsu, Tali, and dearly departed Meronym. Without their support and cuddles this book could not have been finished. Finally, reader, we want to thank you for the work you have done during these impossible times. While we are the two who wrote it, we all lived it.

NOTES

Foreword

[1] Elisabeth Kubler-Ross and David Kessler, *On Grief and Grieving: Finding the Meaning of Grief through the Five Stages of Loss* (New York: Scribner, 2005), 7.

Introduction

[1] Dessa, "Good Grief," track 5 on *Chime*, DoomTree Records, released February 23, 2018.

[2] Larisa A. Garski and Justine Mastin, *Starship Therapise: Using Therapeutic Fanfiction to Rewrite Your Life* (Berkley, CA: North Atlantic Books, 2021), 81–91.

1. The Realm of Our Plague

[1] Michael White, *Maps of Narrative Practice* (New York & London: W.W. Norton & Company, 2007), 1.

[2] White, *Maps*.

[3] Larisa Garski and Justine Mastin, "Beyond Canon: Therapeutic Fanfiction and the Queer Hero's Journey," in *Using Superheroes and Villains in Counseling and*

Play Therapy, ed. Lawrence C. Ruben (New York: Routledge, 2020), 264–73.

[4] Felicity Callard and Elisa Perego, "How and Why Patients Made Long Covid," *Social Science & Medicine* 268 (2021): 113426, doi.org/10.1016/j.socscimed.2020.113426.

2. The Realm of Our Health

[1] Audre Lorde, *A Burst of Light and Other Essays* (Mineola: Ixia Press, 2017), 44, iBooks.
[2] Audre Lorde, *The Cancer Journals* (New York: Penguin Books 2020), 16, iBooks.
[3] Meghan O'Rourke, *The Invisible Kingdom* (New York: Riverhead Books, 2022), 10–11, iBooks.
[4] Lorde, *Cancer Journals*.
[5] Lorde, *Cancer Journals*, 13.
[6] "A Guide to Disability Rights Laws," Disability Rights Section, Civil Rights Division, US Department of Justice, February 2020, https://www.ada.gov/cguide.htm.
[7] Derek H. Suite, Robert La Bril, Annelle Primm, and Phyllis Harrison-Ross, "Beyond Misdiagnosis, Misunderstanding and Mistrust: Relevance of the Historical

Perspective in the Medical and Mental Health Treatment of People of Color," *Journal of the National Medical Association* 99, no.8 (2007): 879–85.

[8] Lorde, *Cancer Journals*, 33.
[9] Kate Bowler, *No Cure for Being Human (and Other Truths I Need to Hear)* (New York: Random House, 2021), 15–16.
[10] Lorde, *Cancer Journals*, 24.
[11] Bessel van der Kolk, *The Body Keeps the Score* (New York: Penguin Books, 2014), 89–104.

3. The Realm of Our Earth

[1] *Cosmos: A Personal Voyage*, episode 1, "The Shores of the Cosmic Ocean," directed by Adrian Malone, aired September 28, 1980, on PBS.
[2] Ivan Boszormenyi-Nagy, *Foundation of Contextual Therapy: Collected Papers of Ivan Boszormenyi-Nagy, M.D.* (New York: Brunner/Mazel, 1987), 321.
[3] T.M. Scanlon, *What We Owe Each Other* (Cambridge & London: Belknap Press of Harvard University, 2000), 189–320.
[4] Teresa McDowell, Carmen Knudson-Martin, and J. Maria Bermudez,

Socioculturally Attuned Family Therapy (New York: Routledge, 2018), 140.

[5] Katharine Hahoe, *Saving Us: A Climate Scientist's Case for Hope and Healing in a Divided World* (New York: One Signal Publishing Atria, 2021), 147–73, iBooks.

[6] Carl R. Rogers, "The Necessary and Sufficient Conditions of Therapeutic Personality Change," *Journal of Counseling Psychology* 21, no.2 (1957): 95–103. doi.org/10.1037/h0045357.

[7] WahinkpeTopa (Four Arrows) and Darcia Narvaez, *Restoring the Kinship Worldview: Indigenous Voices Introduce 28 Precepts for Rebalancing Life on Planet Earth* (Berkeley, CA: North Atlantic Books, 2022), 1–30.

[8] "UN Chief Warns against 'Sleepwalking to Climate Catastrophe,'" *UN News*, March 21, 2022, https://news.un.org/en/story/2022/03/1114322.

[9] Emily Nagoski and Amelia Nagoski, *Burnout: The Secret to Unlocking the Stress Cycle* (New York: Ballantine Books, 2019), 20–21, iBooks.

[10] Nagoski and Nagoski, *Burnout*, 19.

[11] David Gleicher, *The Rescue of the Third Class on the Titanic: A Revisionist History* (Liverpool, UK: Liverpool University Press, 2006), 13–15.

[12] *Titanic: Band of Courage*, directed by Donald Baret, 2014, PBS.

[13] Christopher Ward, *And the Band Played On* (London: Hodder & Stoughton, 2011), 1.

[14] Ward, *And the Band*, 4.

[15] Risa Dickens and Amy Torok, *Missing Witches: Recovering the True Histories of Feminist Magic* (Berkeley, CA: North Atlantic Books, 2021), 80–136, 140–54.

4. The Realm of Our Origins

[1] Pauline Boss, *The Myth of Closure: Ambiguous Loss in a Time of Pandemic and Change* (New York & London: W.W. Norton & Company, 2021), 17, iBooks.

[2] Carl Whitaker, *Midnight Musings of a Family Therapist*, ed. Margaret O. Ryan (New York & London: W.W. Norton & Company, 1989), 176–223.

[3] Boss, *Myth of Closure*, 17.

[4] Richard C. Schwartz, "Moving from Acceptance toward Transformation with Internal Family Systems Therapy (IFS)," *Journal of Clinical Psychology* 69, no.8 (2013): 805–17.

[5] Richard C. Schwartz and Martha Sweezy, *Internal Family Systems Therapy* (New York and London: Guilford Press, 2020), 31–39.

[6] Jamie Marich, *Dissociation Made Simple: A Stigma-Free Guide to Embracing Your Dissociative Mind and Navigating Daily Life* (Berkeley, CA: North Atlantic Books, 2023), 26–28.

[7] Mark Wolynn, *It Didn't Start with Me* (New York: Penguin Books, 2016), 15–40.

[8] Murray Bowen, *Family Therapy in Clinical Practice* (Lanham, MD: Rowman & Littlefield Publishers, 2004), 467–534.

[9] Tom Holmes with Lauri Holmes, *Parts Work: An Illustrated Guide to Your Inner Life* (Kalamazoo, MI: Winged Heart Press, 2007), 31–41.

[10] Pauling Boss, *Ambiguous Loss: Learning to Live with Unresolved Grief* (Cambridge, MA: Harvard University Press, 1999), 4–5.

[11] Boss, *Myth of Closure*, 17–18.

[12] Boss, *Myth of Closure*, 26.

[13] Frank G. Anderson, Martha Sweezy, and Richard C. Schwartz, *Internal Family Systems Skills Training Manual* (Eau Claire, WI: PESI Publishing & Media, 2017), 33.

[14] Boss, *Myth of Closure*, 36.

[15] Boss, *Myth of Closure*, 17.

[16] *Supernatural,* season 5, episode 22, "Swan Song," directed by Steve Boyum, featuring Jared Padalecki, Jensen Ackels, and Mischa Collins, aired May 13, 2010, in broadcast syndication, Warner Bros. Television.

5. The Realm of Our Kin

[1] Harry J. Aponte and Karni Kissil, *The Person of the Therapist Training Model: Mastering the Use of Self* (New York: Routledge, 2016), 4.

[2] Curt Widhalm and Katie Vernoy, "The Person of the Therapist: An Interview with Dr. Harry Aponte," May 11, 2020, in *Modern Therapist's Survival Guide,* podcast, https://therapyreimagined.com/modern-therapist-podcast/the-person-of-the-therapist/.

[3] Widhalm and Vernoy, "Person of the Therapist."

[4] Aponte and Kissil, *Person of the Therapist,* 1–12.

[5] Widhalm and Vernoy, "Person of the Therapist."

[6] Britt Holewinski, "Underground Networking: The Amazing Connections beneath Your Feet," National Forest Foundation, accessed August 22, 2022, ht

[continued] tps://www.nationalforests.org/blog/underground-mycorrhizal-network.

[7] WahinkpeTopa (Four Arrows) and Darcia Narvaez, *Restoring the Kinship Worldview: Indigenous Voices Introduce 28 Precepts for Rebalancing Life on Planet Earth* (Berkeley, CA: North Atlantic Books, 2022), 1–30.

[8] Richard C. Schwartz and Martha Sweezy, *Internal Family Systems Therapy* (New York and London: Guilford Press, 2020), 56–58.

[9] Widhalm and Vernoy, "Person of the Therapist."

[10] Harry J. Aponte and J. Carol Carlsen, "An Instrument for Person-of-the-Therapist Supervision," *Journal of Marital and Family Therapy* 35, no.4 (2009): 395–405, https://doi.org/10.1111/j.1752-0606.2009.00127.x.

6. The Realm of Our Republic

[1] Byung-Chul Han, *The Expulsion of the Other* (Cambridge, UK: Polity Press, 2018), 108, iBooks.

[2] Elisabeth Kubler-Ross and David Kessler, *On Grief and Grieving* (New York: Scribner, 2014), 7–28.

[3] David Kessler, *Finding Meaning: The Sixth Stage of Grief* (New York: Scribner, 2019), 67–81.

[4] Byung-Chul Han, *Capitalism and the Death Drive*, trans. Daniel Steuer (Cambridge, UK: Polity Press, 2021), 1–14, iBooks.

[5] Byung-Chul Han, *The Palliative Society*, trans. Daniel Steuer (Cambridge, UK: Polity Press, 2021), 10–15, iBooks.

[6] Han, *Palliative Society*, 6.

[7] Han, *Expulsion*, 110–11.

[8] Elisabeth Kubler-Ross, *On Death and Dying: What the Dying Have to Teach Doctors, Nurses, Clergy, and Their Own Families* (New York: Scribner, 2014), 49–78.

[9] Kubler-Ross and Kessler, *Grief*, 16.

[10] Kessler, *Finding Meaning*, 67–81.

[11] *The Collected Works of C.G. Jung*, ed. Herbert Read, Michael Fordham, Gerhard Adler, and William McGuire, vol.7, *Two Essays in Analytical Psychology*, trans. R.F.C. Hull (Princeton, NJ: Princeton University Press, 1959), 5873, iBooks.

7. The Realm of Our Faith

[1] Thich Nhat Hanh, *Going Home: Jesus and Buddha as Brothers* (New York: Riverhead Books, 2000), 56.

[2] Risa Dickens and Amy Torok, *Missing Witches: Recovering the True Histories of Feminist Magic* (Berkeley, CA: North Atlantic Books, 2021), 232–56.

[3] Thich Nhat Hanh, *The World We Have: A Buddhist Approach to Peace and Ecology* (Berkeley, CA: Parallax Press, 2008), vii.

[4] Byung-Chul Han, *The Burnout Society* (Stanford, CA: Stanford University Press, 2015), 30, iBooks.

[5] Thich Nhat Hanh, *The Miracle of Mindfulness: An Introduction to the Practice of Meditation*, trans. Mobi Ho (Boston: Beacon Press, 1987), 14.

[6] Manfred F.R. Kets de Vries, "The Shaman, the Therapist, and the Coach," *Organizational and Social Dynamics* 16, no.1 (2016): 1–18. https://doi.org/10.2139/ssrn.2503413.

[7] Thich Nhat Hanh, *You Are Here: Discovering the Magic of the Present Moment*, ed. Melvin McLeod, trans. Sherab Chödzin Kohn (Boston & London: Shambhala, 2010), 107.

[8] Larisa A. Garski and Justine Mastin, *Starship Therapise: Using Therapeutic Fanfiction to Rewrite Your Life* (Berkeley, CA: North Atlantic Books, 2021), 81–95.

8. The Realm of Our Crisis

[1] Kaira Jewel Lingo, *We Were Made for These Times: Ten Lessons on Moving through Change, Loss, and Disruption* (Berkeley, CA: Parallax Press, 2021), 28.
[2] Lingo, *Made for These Times*, 3–4.
[3] Lingo, *Made for These Times*, 55.
[4] Lingo, *Made for These Times*, 55.
[5] Lingo, *Made for These Times*, 65–66.
[6] Casper Ter Kuile, *The Power of Ritual: Turning Everyday Activities into Soulful Practices* (New York: HarperCollins, 2020), 173.

9. The Realm of Our Industry

[1] Bruce Minor dispensed this wisdom during a training that Larisa took from him in Minneapolis in 2016.
[2] Sharon Klayman Farber, "The Overt and Covert Freud: Prototype of the Wounded Healer," in *Celebrating the Wounded Healer: Pain, Post-traumatic Growth, and Self-Disclosure*, ed. Sharon Klayman Farber

(London and New York: Routledge, 2017), 195–305, iBooks.

[3] John Kerr, *A Most Dangerous Method: The Story of Jung, Freud, and Sabina Spielrein* (New York: Alfred A. Knopf, 1993), 441–503.

[4] Kashmir Hill and Aaron Krolik, "At Talkspace, Start-Up Culture Collides with Mental Health Concerns," *New York Times*, August 7, 2020, https://www.nytimes.com/2020/08/07/technology/talkspace.html.

[5] Emily Nagoski and Amelia Nagoski, *Burnout: The Secret to Unlocking the Stress Cycle* (New York: Ballantine Books, 2019), 8–21, iBooks.

[6] Jonathan Shay, "Moral Injury," *Psychoanalytic Psychology* 31, no.2 (2014): 183.

[7] Wendy Dean, Simon Talbot, and Austin Dean, "Reframing Clinician Distress: Moral Injury Not Burnout," *Federal Practitioner* 36, no.9 (2019): 400–402.

10. The Realm of Our Meaning

[1] Rutger Bregman, *Utopia for Realists: How We Can Build the Ideal World*, trans. Elizabeth Manton (New York: Back Bay Books, 2017), 9–30.

[2] Rutger Bregman, *Humankind: A Hopeful History*, trans. Elizabeth Manton and Erica Moore (New York: Little, Brown and Company, 2021), 1–134.

[3] Delan Bruce, "Afrofuturism: From the Past to the Living Present," *UCLA Newsroom*, September 20, 2020, https://newsroom.ucla.edu/magazine/afrofuturism.

ABOUT THE AUTHORS

Larisa A. Garski, LMFT, and Justine Mastin, LMFT, LADC, met while they were in graduate school and have been coconspirators ever since. They literally wrote the book on Therapeutic Fanfiction—*Starship Therapise: Using Therapeutic Fanfiction to Rewrite Your Life* —and they're also research partners and co-chapter authors in numerous pop culture psychology texts, including: *Supernatural Psychology: Roads Less Traveled*, *Daredevil Psychology: The Devil You Know*, *Westworld Psychology: Violent Delights*, *The Psychology of Zelda*, *Black Panther Psychology: Hidden Kingdoms*, *The Joker Psychology: Evil Clowns and the Women Who Love Them*, and *Stranger Things Psychology: Life Upside Down*. Additionally, they contributed chapters to the academic text *Using Superheroes and Villains in Counseling and Play Therapy: A Guide for Mental Health Professionals*. Justine also wrote the foreword to JSalvador's *Super Emo Friends: a decade of depression* and contributed an essay to the compilation *Embodied Resilience through Yoga: 30 Mindful Essays About Finding Empowerment After Addiction, Trauma, Grief, and Loss*. Justine and Larisa cohost the *Starship Therapise* podcast, where they make difficult psychological concepts relatable through the lens of pop culture. Their individual and collaborative work in the wellness field has been covered by such outlets as *The Wall Street Journal, SELF, Forbes, Yoga International,*

Health Central, *Shondaland*, and *Bustle*. Justine and Larisa are both AAMFT-Approved Supervisors.

Larisa A. Garski, LMFT, is a psychotherapist and the chief of clinical staff at Empowered Therapy in Chicago, Illinois. She specializes in working with women, families, and young adults who identify as outside the mainstream, such as those in the geek and LGBTQIA+ communities.

Justine Mastin, LMFT, LADC, is the owner/founder of Blue Box Counseling and Wellness in Minneapolis, Minnesota. She is also an adjunct instructor for marriage and family therapy graduate students at Saint Mary's

University of Minnesota and University of Massachusetts Global.

About North Atlantic Books

North Atlantic Books (NAB) is an independent, nonprofit publisher committed to a bold exploration of the relationships between mind, body, spirit, and nature. Founded in 1974, NAB aims to nurture a holistic view of the arts, sciences, humanities, and healing. To make a donation or to learn more about our books, authors, events, and newsletter, please visit www.northatlanticbooks.com.

BACK COVER MATERIAL

How do you practice good therapy when it's the end of the world ... and no one feels fine? What can you do when you're navigating the same existential crises and big unknowns that your clients turn to you to help make sense of?

In *The Grieving Therapist,* psychotherapists Larisa A. Garski, LMFT, and Justine Mastin, LMFT, give voice to the difficulties of therapising in today's world—and offer a grief-informed framework for taking care of yourself as you take care of others.

Informed by narrative therapy, Internal Family Systems (IFS), fanfic, and trauma-sensitive therapy, Garski and Mastin examine what it means to be a therapist at the end of the world (or what feels like it). They break down the 10 realms of grief that are critical to understand and work with today but likely weren't taught to you in therapy school. Each chapter includes:

- **Grieving tools** that can be adapted for both client and therapist
- **Tips** for supervisors and supervisees
- **Skills** for maintaining healthy relationships outside the office

- **Support** for current therapy students (and therapists new to the field)
- **Advice** on how to work with clients who are navigating the same issues as you
- **Meditations** on love, life, death, and connection

"Reading this timely book is like having a conversation with the supervisor of your dreams."
—Nicole Arzt, LMFT, author of *Sometimes Therapy Is Awkward*

"With a subtle, engaging, and practical narrative, Garski and Mastin use a medicine wheel format, the wisdom of animals, the meaning-making of ritual, campfire magic, and fearless trust in the universe to bring therapists back to earth. The result is mutual healing for therapists, clients, and the planet."
—Four Arrows, coauthor of *Restoring the Kinship Worldview*

"A much-needed resource for all therapists—a timely reminder that we are all human, we all grieve, and we all need to heal together."
—Janina Scarlet, PhD, author of *Superhero Therapy*

Index

A

acceptance, *47, 101, 124, 132, 185, 194*
accommodations, *209, 211*
acknowledgment,
  of COVID pandemic pain, *18, 20*
  of each part, *82, 85*
  of struggles for disabled people, *49, 50*
  of systemic influences, *113*
  of town crier, *67*
action, *199*
activism, intentional, *235, 236, 238, 267, 268*
Adler, Alfred, *217*
Afrofuturists, *252*
ahimsa, *25, 191, 193*
alcohol treatment, *218*
alone, being, *184*
ambiguous loss, *86, 96*
American culture,
  as capitalist, *61, 128, 238, 247*
  crises in, *197, 198*
  and government, *112*
  grieving oppressive, *142, 143*
  loss of rights in, *137*
  myth of autonomy in, *145, 146*
  post-2016 presidential election, *135*
  time norms in, *128*
anxiety, *20, 58, 60, 183, 238*
Aponte, Dr. Harry, *104, 111, 126, 128*
app therapy, *221, 222, 224, 225*
art, *148, 162, 232*
avoidance, *111*

B

beliefs, *140, 142, 175, 176, 177, 179*
  See also religion,
BIPOC community,
  Afrofuturists' vision for, *252*

collective trauma in, *211, 212*
COVID-19 pandemic effects, *15*
crises in, *193*
health-care inequalities for, *33, 35*
body, the,
care for, *52*
experiential learning about, *46, 47*
'healthy' body type, *36*
mind/body relationship, *43, 44, 46*
as political, *152*
in school, *49, 50, 52*
sitting with the present, *44, 46*
social messages about, *44*
Boss, Pauline, *86, 100*
Boszormenyi-Nagy, Ivan, *54*
both/and thinking, *91*
boundaries, *97, 202, 208, 211, 225, 236*
Bowen, Murray, *85, 105, 136*
brain fog, *12*
breath, *15, 61, 245*
Bregman, Rutger, *248*
Buddhism, *162, 166, 199*
burdens, legacy, *108, 109, 111*
burnout, *64, 65, 225, 227, 228, 230, 231, 239, 240, 242, 243*
Byung-Chul Han, *140, 154*

C

call-ins/call-outs, *198*
capitalist society, *61, 118, 128, 238, 247*
care,
coordination, *219, 221*
for/by our kin, *118, 119*
self-care, *52, 65, 240*
caregivers,
common pitfalls of,
lack of support for, *119*
support systems for, *9*
therapists as, *238, 239*
change,
death of a dream, *227*
hard work of, *215, 230, 231, 257, 258*
healing via, *251*
imagining, *251, 261, 262, 265, 267, 268, 269*

life, *243, 245*
  one-on-one acts of, *143*
  reflection vs., *18*
  slowness of, *254*
  to sustain the Earth, *64*
children, *43, 123*
chosen family.,
  See kin,
clients,
  bodily experiences of, *50, 52*
  'bringing home', *148*
  do no harm to, *191, 193*
  Earth as, *56, 57, 58, 60*
  faith tools for, *176, 177*
  family of origin reflected in, *99*
  grieving illnesses, *42*
  industry stakeholders vs., *228, 230*
  mirroring for, *201, 202*
  need for the neutral zone, *18*
  overexplaining by, *121, 122*
  pain paradox for, *232, 233*
  political divisions with, *135, 136*
  quality, not quantity of, *252, 254*
  return-to-sender tool for, *92, 93*
  social modeling for, *193*
  tea with their shadow, *146, 147*
  as town criers, *64, 65*
climate change,
  acknowledging, *71, 72, 74*
  differing effects of, *61*
  reality of, *58, 60*
  therapy amidst, *75, 76*
cognitive dissonance, *88*
collective trauma,
  about the Earth, *74, 75*
  in the classroom, *129, 211, 212, 243*
  grieving, *227, 228*
  individual crisis and, *193*
community,
  asking needs of, *111, 112*
  chosen, *104, 258*

communal living, *118*
of COVID-era therapists, *3*
fear of being cast out of, *137*
gift of, *269, 270*
grieving in, *10, 74*
in healing journey, *104, 105, 255*
hierarchy vs., *219, 221*
as human nature, *6*
need for, *249*
in-person, *225*
radically divergent, *139*
spiritual principle of, *180*

compartmentalization, *18, 44, 137, 191*

compassion,
for ambiguous loss, *227*
around family member death/loss, *101*
via both/and thinking, *91*
for Earth, *62*
emotional, *194*
enmeshment and, *91, 93*
gift of, *270*
over COVID, *13, 15, 16*
and political divisiveness, *135, 136*
self-, *9, 23, 52, 99*
for your shadow, *148, 150*

connection,
complicated web of, *107, 108*
emotional, *6, 7*
human/cosmic, *54, 56*
human/Earth, *58, 60, 61, 258*
kinship ties, *115, 117, 118, 119*
religion/spirituality as voicing, *172*
vs. separation, *85*

contextual family therapy, *54*

control, loss of, *197, 198*

conversation,
about crises, *198, 207, 208, 209*
about negative self-talk, *44, 46*
authentic political, *155, 157*
vs. change of action, *18*

COVID-centric, *20*
honest, with students, *268, 269*
with our shadow, *146, 147*
overexplaining, *121, 122, 123*
Self/Other, *139, 140, 142, 143, 145, 154*
verbalize to normalize, *23, 76, 117*
countertransference, *67, 96*
couples therapy, *122*
COVID-19 pandemic,
  both/and thinking about, *91*
  chronic illness and, *32*
  fear of, *10, 12*
  grief and fatigue from, *18, 20, 21*
  lack of knowledge about, *12, 13*
  minimizing, *13*
  mourning the losses of, *9, 10, 18, 20*
  panic over, *190*
  in-person work during, *7, 9, 10*
  reaction to mandates in, *146, 147*
  solo sojourns during, *1*
  supervisees/supervisors in, *21, 23*
  telehealth, *3, 5, 6, 7*
  therapeutic tools for, *16, 18*
  worker-bee response to,
creativity, *40, 42, 197, 232, 233, 260*
crises,
  acceptance of, *185*
  collective and individual, *193, 197, 198*
  coping with, *187, 188, 190, 195*
  disclosing, *207, 208*
  five remembrances for, *199*
  interpersonal collisions from, *197, 198*
  management, *195, 197, 198, 199*
  mirroring tool for, *201, 202, 203*

preparation for, *190, 191*

signs of, *191*

wisdom via, *255*

witness vs victims of, *195*

crying, *97*

curiosity, *255*

cutting off relationships, *136*

D

D'Angelo, Ginny, *215*

danger, *64, 65*

death,

ambiguous loss in, *86*

and change, *262*

of chosen kin, *130*

of a family member, *100, 101, 102*

five remembrances on, *199, 260*

gratitude in change and, *245*

illness as reminder of, *38, 39, 52*

meaning-making in, *170, 172*

pain of grieving, *25*

as part of life, *163*

preparation for, *184, 260*

and rebirth, *251*

Utopia as including, *269*

See also loss,

death/love relationship,

chronic illness and, *52*

climate change and, *76, 77*

crisis and the, *212*

effect of COVID pandemic on, *24, 25, 27*

faith and, *184*

family-of-origin work and, *100, 101, 102*

kinship network and, *130*

navigating political differences, *158, 159*

deconstructing faith, *175, 176, 177, 179*

denial, *33*

dialectical relationships, *36, 38*

differentiation, *85, 136*

disability/disabled people,

accommodating, *49, 50, 52*
  COVID and, *13*
  disability defined, *33*
  in the education system, *49, 50, 52*
  legal marriage for, *115, 117*
  self-advocacy by, *49, 50*
  as 'shameful', *35, 36*
  training on, *46*
  See also illness, chronic,
disownment, *137*
dissociation, *191, 199*
dissonance, generational, *86, 88, 89, 91*
distress tolerance, *47, 232*
doctorate degrees, *219, 221*
double binds, *230, 235*
dream, death of a, *21, 27, 227, 242*
drug and alcohol treatment, *218*

E

Earth,
  communal perspective of, *60, 61, 62*
  dependence on/collaboration with, *60, 61, 77*
  life choices on, *69, 71*
  needs/struggles of, *56, 57, 58, 60*
  training therapists for work on, *76*
education,
  about the body, *47*
  chronic illness and, *49, 50, 52*
  climate change and, *74, 75, 76*
  during the COVID pandemic, *23, 24*
  crisis management and, *209, 211, 212*
  family-of-origin work, *99, 100*
  kinship network in, *128, 129*
  navigating politics during, *157, 158*
  pay based on, *219*
  reimagining system of, *268, 269*

on religion and philosophy, *183, 184*
  theory/practice balance, *242, 243*
  therapy industry and, *240, 242, 243*
emergencies, *92, 93*
emotional connection, *6, 7*
emotions.,
  See feelings,
empathy, *7, 91, 194*
energy,
  COVID-era sapping of, *121*
  exhausting emotional, *25, 122, 157*
  to face climate crisis, *72, 74, 75*
  to foster relationships, *124*
  for our own feelings, *111*
  for political discussion, *142, 152*
  Self energy, *85, 96, 129*
enmeshment, *91*
'enough' being, *254*
Epston, David, *1, 10*

equity, *57*
existential questions, *60, 168, 169, 183*
exit strategies, *222*
expectations, managing, *225*
experiential family therapy, *79*

F

fairness,
  in Afrofuturist world, *252*
  burdens on therapists, *145*
  grieving injustice, *143*
  of serving when in crisis, *195*
  in the therapy industry, *239*
  in treatment of Earth, *57*
faith.,
  See religion; spirituality,
faith, deconstructing, *175*
family, chosen.,
  See kin,
family of origin,

appearance as parts, *89*
and chosen kin, *107, 117, 118*
clients' reflection of, *99*
countertransference and, *96, 97*
death/loss within, *100, 101, 102*
generational dissonance, *86, 88, 89, 91*
gratitude for, *258*
health and, *36*
impact of, *83, 85, 89*
as inexorable, *80, 89*
in Internal Family Systems, *82, 83, 85, 88, 100*
passing traits back/forward, *102*
return-to-sender tool, *91, 92, 93, 94, 102*
family therapy., See marriage and family therapy (MFT),
fandom characters, *174, 179*
Fanfiction, Therapeutic., See Therapeutic Fanfiction,
fatigue, *9, 12, 20, 21*
feelings,
   about climate change, *60*
   anger, *143, 146*
   around family member death/loss, *101*
   avoiding overwhelming, *46*
   being present with, *57, 58, 197, 212*
   bringing home, *148*
   enmeshment of, *91, 92, 93*
   expression of, *97, 201*
   fear, *12, 71, 72, 190*
   neutral zone for noticing, *18*
   panic, *190, 191*
   parts work with, *194*
   resentment, *57, 58*
   in stages of grief, *143, 152*
   therapy as realm of, *227*
   towards our shadow, *147, 148*

turned against each other, *24*
five remembrances, *199*
Floyd, Mr. George, *155, 193*
Freud, Sigmund, *217*
friendships, *117, 124*
future, fanficcing, *261, 262*

G

generational dissonance, *86, 88, 89, 91, 99*
genograms, *126*
gifts,
    of illness, *39, 40, 42*
    of listening, *140*
    of remembering death, *199, 260*
    spiritual, *181*
    of wisdom, *257*
government, American, *112*
    See also politics,
gratitude,
    via focus on impermanence, *199*
    for past relationships, *124*
    for this moment, *245*
    for wisdom, *258*
grief,
    about cutting off clients, *136*
    about Earth, *72, 74*
    about kinship ties, *119*
    about leaves of absence, *197*
    about legacy burdens, *111*
    about the body, *44, 46*
    ambiguous, *101*
    avoiding, *111*
    in community, *10, 142, 143, 203*
    death of a dream, *21, 27, 227*
    within families, *100, 101, 102*
    finding allies in, *74*
    healing change via, *251*
    limitations of illness, *42*
    as love persevering, *25, 27*
    maps for, *1*
    as non-linear,
    six stages of, *132, 152, 158*

from sudden, tragic loss, *212*
supports for, of systematic oppression, *142, 143*
when relationships change, *124*
grieving tools,
defining limits, *40, 42, 43*
fanficcing the future, *261, 262*
neutral zone, *16, 18*
overexplaining, *121, 122, 123*
pain paradox, *231, 232, 233, 235*
reduce, reuse, renew, *175, 176, 177, 179*
resources for grief,
return to sender, *91, 92, 93, 94, 102*
social modeling, *201, 202, 203*
tea with your shadow, *145, 146, 147, 148, 150*
town crier, *64, 65, 67*
growth, *152*
guilt, *7, 9, 47, 136, 205*

H

harm, do no, *25, 191, 193, 228*
harm reduction, *235, 236, 239*
healing,
around death, *100*
via change, *251*
within family/community, *105*
learning/needing, *76*
via listening, *140*
via meaning-making, *231, 233*
pain paradox and, *232, 233*
via religion/spirituality, *174*
health,
constraints on caring for, *42*
'healthy' body type, *32, 33, 36*
wellness/illness relationship, *32, 33, 35, 36, 38*
helping professions, *9, 230, 239*

helping yourself first, *203, 222*
hero's journey, *172*
hero/savior/sacrifice syndrome, *231*
hierarchy vs. community, *221*
home life/work like, *118, 148, 233*
homeostasis, *108*
honesty, *191*
hope, *269, 270*
human beings,
    crisis as inevitable for, *199*
    effect on Earth, *57*
    God as image of, *160*
    needs of, *208*
    as parts and Self, *52, 82*
    systemic influences on, *154*
Humankind: A Hopeful History (Bregman), *248*

I

identity, *35, 146, 152, 158, 193*
illness, chronic,
    Audre Lorde's advocacy for, *29*
    grieving limits of, *42*
    hidden or invisible, *35, 36*
    pain of, *38, 39*
    physical 'look' of, *32, 33*
    as reminder of mortality, *39, 52*
    as 'shameful', *33, 36*
    strength and, *30*
    wellness/illness relationship, *32, 33, 35, 36, 38*
imagination, *251, 252, 254, 255*
immunocompromise, *9, 13, 43*
impermanence, *199*
income,
    for care, *236, 238, 239*
    education and, *219*
    health and, *36*
    during licensure, *221, 222*
    third-party control of, *218, 219, 242, 243*
individual crisis, *193*
industry, therapy,

app therapy, *221, 222, 224, 225*
  beginnings of, *217*
  burnout and moral injury in, *228, 230, 235, 239, 240, 242, 243*
  career changes in, *245*
  changing norms in, *218*
  insurance, *218, 219, 236, 238*
  licensure, *219, 221*
  pain paradox in, *231, 232, 233, 235*
  reimagining values for, *252*
  self of the therapist in, *235, 236, 238, 239*
  third-party control of, *218, 219*
informed consent, *142*
in-home therapy, *205, 209, 222*
injury, moral, *225, 227, 228, 230, 231*
injustice, *64*
inner work, *43, 82*
in-person therapy, *6, 7, 9, 10, 245*

insurance, *218, 219, 236, 238, 242, 267, 268*
integration, *140*
Internal Family Systems (IFS),
  choosing Self energy, *152*
  and chosen kin, *108*
  in crisis, *191*
  defined, *82*
  exiles in, *145*
  getting to know, *100, 258*
  holding dissimilar parts, *148, 150*
  as inexorable, *94, 101, 136*
  ingrained norms of, *117*
  parts work with, *83*
internships, free, *240, 242*
intersectionality, *60, 61, 193, 198*
invisibility,
  of chronic illness/pain, *35, 36*
  of kinship networks, *115*
  legacy burden of, *109*

isolation, *10*

J
Jung, Carl, *145, 217*

K
kin,
    care for/by, *118, 119*
    as chosen family, *104*
    family of origin blended with, *117, 118*
    genograms of, *126*
    healing within sphere of, *105*
    legacy burdens within, *108, 109, 111*
    neighborhood networks, *115*
    non-normative connections, *115, 117*
    nurturing/relinquishing relations, *123, 124*
    overexplaining to, *121, 122, 123*
    pets as, *130*
    reasons for choosing, *108*
    systemic influences, *111, 112, 113*
    temporary, *128, 129*

Kübler-Ross, Elisabeth, *132, 142, 143, 158*

L
leadership, *23, 169*
legacy burdens, *108, 109, 111, 112, 113*
Libi, Michelle, *215*
licensure, *219, 221, 222*
life,
    changing your, *185, 243, 245*
    of doing what you love, *69, 71*
    imagining a new, *247, 251, 252, 254, 255*
    impermanence of, *199*
    pain in, *38, 39*
    tree of your, *107, 108*
limits, defining, *40, 42, 43, 197, 218*
Lingo, Kaira Jewel, *185, 194, 199*
listening, *140*
lockdown, COVID-, *6, 16*
long COVID, *12*
Lorde, Audre, *29, 35*
loss,

ambiguous, *86, 96, 158, 227*
  of control, *197, 198*
  of a family member, *100, 101, 102*
  five remembrances for, *199, 260*
  gratitude in change and, *245*
  healing change via, *251*
  insights from, *123*
  sudden, tragic, *212*
love, *25, 27, 251, 260*
  See also death/love relationship,

M

map making,
  in community, *10, 27*
  for the future, *251*
  for grief, *1*
marginalization,
  collective trauma and, *193*
  religious, *168*
  treatment for illness and, *33, 35*
marriage, legal, *115, 117, 119*

marriage and family therapy (MFT),
  contextual, *54*
  in-home, *205, 222*
  mentors in, *79, 80, 104, 215*
  structural, *105*
martyr complex, *231*
McClintock, Harry, *247*
meaning-making,
  to craft Utopia, *255, 257, 258, 260, 261*
  following anger, *143*
  healing via, *176*
  includes pain, *231, 233, 269*
  practices, *179*
  reimagining values for, *251, 252, 254, 255, 264*
  via religion, *162, 165, 168, 169*
  via service, *254*
  via spirituality, *169, 170, 184*
  via therapy, *168*
  via understanding, *255*
memento mori, *199, 260*
mentors, *214, 215*
Meronym, *130*

Miller, Briar, *215*
mind/body relationship, *43, 44, 46, 47*
mindfulness, *160, 166, 180, 194*
Minor, Bruce, *214, 215, 217*
Minuchin, Sal, *105*
mirror neurons, *201, 202*
miscommunication, *121, 122*
modeling emotions, *201, 202, 203*
moral injury, *225, 227, 228, 230, 231, 235, 239, 240, 242, 243*
morality, *33, 52*
mourning,
    COVID losses, *9, 10, 18, 20*
    and present-time love, *212*
    See also grief,
mythologies, modern, *179*

N

Nagoski, Amelia and Emily, *67*
naming things,
    distress, *71, 72*
    in the neutral zone, *18*

overexplaining and, *121, 122, 123*
power in, *74*
narrative therapy, *1, 208*
natural resources, *61*
nature, *179, 180*
negative self-talk, *44, 46*
neighborhood kinship, *115, 117, 118, 119*
neoliberalism, *132*
nervous systems, *6, 24, 190, 199*
neutral zone, *16, 39*
nihilism, *69*
nonattachment, *166*

O

observation,
    of countertransference, *96*
    of dangers, *65*
    of each part, *85*
    of legacy burdens, *109*
    in the neutral zone, *16, 18*
    See also reflection time,

oppression, systemic, *142, 168, 176*
'other',
  chronic illness as, *38*
  enslavement of, *112*
  pain of presence with, *137*
  Self/Other conversation, *139, 140, 142, 143, 145, 154*
overexplaining, *121, 122, 123*
overwhelm,
  attempts to transfer, *92, 93*
  breath for, *61*
  in capitalist society, *118*
  by climate change, *60*
  neutral zone for, *18*
  by political engagement, *145*
  signs of, *191, 193*
  support for, *46*
overworking,
  common pitfall of, in the face of crisis, *190, 195*
  vs. retired ease, *264*

P
pain,
  of being in the body, *44*
  of being present with 'other', *137*
  chronic illness and, *38, 39*
  within families, *100, 101, 102*
  in graduate programs, *50*
  of grief/love, *25*
  importance of feeling, *111, 112, 260*
  necessary, *231*
  paradox, *231, 232, 233, 235*
  shared experience of, *203*
  Utopia via facing our, *247, 248*
panic, *190*
parallel processing, *46, 140*
parts,
  choosing which to have present, *85, 86*
  countertransference and, *94, 96*

disagreeable/dissimilar, *136, 137*
   emotions as, *194*
   in faith work, *177*
   as family members, *89*
   hidden, shadow, *145, 146, 147, 148, 150*
   legacy burdens, *108, 109*
   liberal and conservative, *148, 150*
   parts work, *82, 83*
   in relationship, *124*
   welcoming all, *85, 88, 99, 137*
passing traits back/forward, *176, 177*
pay.,
   See income,
peace with grief, *25*
pets, *130*
philosophy, *183, 184*
play therapy,
   sandbox play, *40, 42*
   virtual, *5, 6*
politics,
   divisions within, *132, 135, 136, 137*
   Earth's pain as, *60*
   in education, *157, 158*
   exploring beliefs about, *140*
   grieving, *142, 143, 145, 158, 227, 228*
   honest discussion of, *155, 157, 197, 198*
   post-presidential election, *135*
   Self/Other conversation, *139, 140, 142, 143, 145*
   tea with your shadow tool, *145, 146, 147, 148, 150*
   in the therapy room, *150, 152, 154, 159*
polyamorous relationships, *115, 118, 168*
positive regard, unconditional, *58*
positivity, toxic, *69*
presence, cultivating, *265*
private practice, *219*
privilege, *15, 61*
productivity, *33, 39, 40, 265*
psychoanalysis, *217*
psychology, *183*

Q
QAnon, *91, 165*

R
racism, *15*
Ramage, Dr. Anne, *215, 222*
reality,
  accepting, *185*
  distraction from, *175*
  imagining a new, *247, 251, 252*
reconciliation, *16*
reduce, reuse, renew tool, *175, 176, 177, 179*
reflection time,
  about climate change, *60, 61*
  about kinship roles, *119*
  about political beliefs, *140*
  on good days/bad days, *159*
  via illness, *39*
  as a living process, *162*
  near water, *180*
  neutral zone for, *39*
  noticing energy levels in, *72*
  pain plus, *231*
  on spirituality in therapeutic work, *174*
relational thinking, *18*
relationships,
  authentic Self in, *124*
  death and, *100*
  divisive, *135*
  genetics and environment, *83*
  healing within, *105*
  homeostasis and chosen, *108*
  maintaining, *123, 124*
  neighborhood kinship, *115, 117, 118, 119*
  no dual, *217*
  See also family of origin; kin,
religion,
  to answer existential questions, *183*
  connection as voiced in, *172*
  depth and breadth of, *163, 165*

education about, *183, 184*
fundamentalist, *168*
healing power of, *174*
holding differences in, *160*
leadership via, *169*
reduce, reuse, renew beliefs tool, *175*
role in our lives, *160*
role in therapy space, *166, 168*
science vs., *168*
spirituality and, *169*
resentment, *57, 58*
resources, natural, *61*
retirement, *264*
return-to-sender tool, *91, 92, 93, 94, 102*
Rider-Waite-Smith tarot, *160*
rights, human, *112, 137*
ritual, *27*
Rogers, Carl, *58, 60*
romantic relationships, *115, 117*

S

sacrifice, *193, 231*
safe space, *191, 222*
Sagan, Carl, *54*
sages, wisdom of, *257, 258, 260, 261*
sandbox play, *40, 42*
Satir, Virginia, *242*
scheduling, *235, 236*
science, *168, 172*
Self,
    authentic, *124, 154, 155, 158, 181, 258*
    -led choices, *113, 152, 268*
    in parts work, *82, 83*
    remaining in energy of, *129*
Self/body connection, *43, 44*
Self/Other conversation, *139, 140, 142, 143, 145, 154*
self of the therapist,
    chronic illness and, *43, 44, 46*
    climate change and, *67, 69, 71*
    crisis management for, *203, 205, 207, 208*

effect of COVID pandemic on, *18, 20, 21*
faith and, *179, 180*
family-of-origin work, *94, 96*
as individual and communal, *61, 62*
kinship network for, *123, 124*
navigating politics, *150, 152, 154*
in the therapy industry, *235, 236, 238, 239*
vs. town crier, *67*
Utopia for, *264, 265*
self-advocacy, *49, 50, 111*
self-care, *52, 65, 240*
self-compassion,
about COVID, *23*
around family of origin, *99*
via care for the body, *52*
for caregiver fatigue, *9*
self-disclosure, *97, 126, 202, 207, 208*
session length, *236, 238*

shadow, tea with your, *145, 146, 147, 148, 150*
shamanism, *170*
shame,
about caregiver fatigue, *9*
about cutting off clients, *136*
about the body, *47*
illness as 'shameful', *33, 36*
Shay, Jonathan, *228*
Smith, Pamela Coleman, *160, 162, 169*
social modeling, *155, 181, 193, 201, 202, 203*
social norms,
about relationships, *115, 117*
about the body, *50, 52*
about time, *128*
grieving oppressive, *142, 143*
illness as 'deviation' from, *33, 36*
legacy burdens in, *112*
somatic techniques, *67*
space,
for death, *184*

emotional, *18, 92, 100, 142*
to grieve intergenerational hurt, *101*
holding, vs. enmeshment, *91, 92*
protecting energetic, *72, 74*
safe, *191*
for spiritual connections, *180*
taking reflection time, *39*
via telehealth, *7*
speech, free, *140*
spirituality,
connection as voiced in, *172*
defined, *169*
healing power of, *174*
meaning-making via, *184*
practices of, *179, 180*
in therapeutic work, *177, 179, 180, 181*
as triggering, *160*
Utopia and, *260*
Star Trek, *16, 18*

stereotypes,
of romantic relationships, *115, 117, 118*
weight and illness, *32, 33*
storytelling,
as buffer from reality, *175*
meaning-making via, *170, 172, 179*
stress, *67*
structural family therapy, *105*
struggle, necessary, *231*
students,
amidst climate collapse, *74, 75, 76*
physical limits in, *49, 50*
systemic change by, *268*
virtual education for, *24*
See also education,
Supernatural, *89*
supervisee/supervisor relationship,
climate change and, *71, 72, 74*

COVID challenges for, *21, 23*
crisis plans, *208, 209*
faith and, *180, 181*
family-of-origin work, *96, 97, 99*
healing in, *105*
holding grief in, *265*
kinship network in, *126, 128*
mentorship in, *214, 215*
navigating politics in, *154, 155, 157*
reimagining system for, *265, 267, 268*
in the therapy industry, *239, 240*
work with chronic illness, *43, 44, 46*
support systems,
    for BIPOC people, *74*
    for caregivers, *9*
    for climate grief, *74*
    in crisis, *205, 207*
    imagining a life with, *251, 265*
    self-advocacy, *49, 50*
systemic burnout, *228*
systemic influences,
America's legacy burden, *111, 112, 113*
dismantling/reimagining, *265, 267*
grieving oppressive, *142*
oppression, *142, 176*
therapy industry, *230, 235, 236, 238, 239, 242*

T

The Cancer Journals (Lorde), *29*
talismans, *27, 176, 177*
tarot, *162, 169*
tea with your shadow, *145, 146, 147, 148, 150*
teaching. *See* education
telehealth, *3, 5, 6, 7, 221, 222, 224, 225*
Therapeutic Fanfiction, *174, 261, 262, 267*
therapists,
    app, *222, 224, 225*
    BIPOC, *74*
    as Buddhist, *168*
    burdens on, *145, 238*
    career changes for, *245*

COVID-era work
fatigue, *20, 21*
crisis signs in, *191*
dream job vs. reality, *227*
early career opportunities, *154*
early industry, *217*
emotional expression by, *97, 99*
faith tools for, *177, 179, 180*
family issues, *91*
family-of-origin work by, *99, 100*
as hope merchants, *269*
as human, *xv, 49, 67, 76, 96, 142, 158, 193, 208*
illness among, *30, 32*
leave of absence for, *197*
mirroring for, *201, 202*
moral injury to, *228, 230*
neutral zone for, *18*
new, *21, 25, 27, 221*
overexplaining by, *122, 123*
pain paradox for, *233, 235*
'person of the therapist' model, *112, 126, 128*
return-to-sender tool for, *93, 94*
shifting out of role of, *148*
as spiritual advisors, *168, 169, 170, 172*
as tabula rasa, *76, 139*
tea with your shadow, *147, 148, 150*
as town criers, *65, 67*
true listening by, *140*
See also supervisee/supervisor relationship,
therapy,
app, *221, 222, 224, 225*
canceled for crisis, *191, 205, 207*
with children, *43*
considering death in, *184*
contextual family, *54*
in-home, *205, 209, 222*
home/work transitions, *85*

industry. See industry, therapy intensity of, *227*
meaning-making via, *168*
narrative, *1, 208*
neutral zone in, *18*
play therapy, *9, 40, 42*
politics in, *152*
religion/spirituality in, *166, 170, 172, 174, 175, 181*
scope of practice, *47*
session length, *128, 236, 238*
systemic, *91*
Therapeutic Fanfiction, *174*
virtual, *3, 5, 6, 7, 221, 222, 224, 225, 245*
work with chronic illness, *111*
Thich Nhat Hanh, *160, 162, 166, 172, 180*
time, session, *128*
time, taking. See reflection time Titanic ship, *67, 69, 71*
tools, grieving.,
    See grieving tools,
town crier, *64, 65, 67*
trauma, collective.,
    See collective trauma,
Tree of Life, *107, 119, 123, 124*
trees, *105, 107*
triggering, *67*

U

understanding, *255, 257*
Utopia,
    change and death in, *269*
    crafting, *255, 257, 258, 260, 261*
    via fanficcing the future, *261, 262*
    imagining, *247, 251, 252, 254, 255*
    as process, not destination, *248, 257*
    for therapists, *264, 265*
    as work, *258*

V

vaccination, COVID-19, *15, 16*
validating feelings, *58, 60*
values, *123, 231, 252*
van der Kolk, Bessel, *44*

verbalize to normalize, *23, 76, 117*
virtual education, *24, 157*
virtual therapy, *3, 5, 6, 7, 221, 222, 224, 225, 245*
voice, personal, *113*
vulnerability, *152*

W

WandaVision, *24, 25*
weakness, perceived, *208*
weight, *32, 33, 36*
wellness industrial complex, *36*
Whitaker, Carl, *79, 80, 86, 89, 102, 215*
White, Michael, *1, 10, 208*
wisdom, *255*
work life/home life, *118, 148, 233*

www.ingramcontent.com/pod-product-compliance
Lightning Source LLC
Chambersburg PA
CBHW011719220426
43663CB00018B/2919